LITTLE MISS BURDEN

by Matilda Ibini

samuelfrench.co.uk

ISBN 978-0-573-13017-5
Concordtheatricals.co.uk
Concordtheatricals.com

For Amateur Production Enquiries

United Kingdom and World excluding North America
licensing@concordtheatricals.co.uk
020-7054-7200

Each title is subject to availability from Samuel French, depending upon country of performance.

This playtext was printed before the end of rehearsals and so may differ slightly from the play as performed.

MUSIC USE NOTE

The music parts for this title are available on hire to licensed productions from Samuel French. Fees and conditions of this hire are quoted on application. Sample materials are available on request for perusal prior to application.

USE OF COPYRIGHT MUSIC

A licence issued by Samuel French Ltd to perform this play does not include permission to use the incidental music specified in this copy. Where the place of performance is already licensed by the PERFORMING RIGHT SOCIETY (PRS) a return of the music used must be made to them. If the place of performance is not so licensed then application should be made to the PRS, 2 Pancras Square, London, N1C 4AG. A separate and additional licence from PHONOGRAPHIC PERFORMANCE LTD, 1 Upper James Street, London W1F 9DE (www.ppluk.com) is needed whenever commercial recordings are used.

IMPORTANT BILLING AND CREDIT REQUIREMENTS

If you have obtained performance rights to this title, please refer to your licensing agreement for important billing and credit requirements.

ABOUT THE AUTHOR

Matilda Ibini is an award-winning playwright, screenwriter (and occasional dramaturg) from London. She was awarded a scholarship from BAFTA and Warner Brothers to study a Masters in Playwriting & Screenwriting. She was part of the Royal Court Writers Program and was a member of Soho Theatre's Writers' Alumni Group. She has had residencies at Soho Theatre, BBC Writersroom, was Graeae Theatre's Artist-in-Residence and completed an attachment at the National Theatre Studio.

Her debut play *Muscovado* was produced by BurntOut Theatre, premiered in 2014 and toured the UK in 2015 starting with a run at Theatre503. *Muscovado* subsequently co-won the Alfred Fagon Audience Award. Her radio play *The Grape that Rolled Under the Fridge* was broadcast on BBC Radio 3. Her work has been staged at the Old Vic Theatre, Bush Theatre, Hampstead Theatre Downstairs, National Theatre Shed, St James Theatre, Royal Exchange Manchester, Birmingham Rep, Soho Theatre, Arcola Theatre, Bunker Theatre, Hackney Showroom and Vaults Festival.

AUTHOR'S NOTE

This is my first (of hopefully many more to come) full length play to be published. To help give you some context about the state of the industry when this was published:

Little Miss Burden is my second produced play in a now nine-year career.

Little Miss Burden is in fact the eighth full-length play I've written in those nine years (not including one feature film, one radio play, over twenty short plays and two unproduced TV spec scripts). This information I'm sharing isn't to boast but a reminder to myself to help invalidate my imposter syndrome when it rears its doubting head and to illustrate that taking up writing as a career, you have to be in it for the long haul. And the level of patience it requires you to exercise for many reasons, some for artistic reasons but most for institutional BS reasons. So have a backup plan, keep the job that pays the bills because writing probably won't for some time.

Some hopefully helpful reflections that I've had over the course of writing this play:

1. You will write more plays/scripts that won't get produced than do. And that is ok. The more you write, the more you give yourself the opportunity for your work to be produced.

2. Your career will never be immune from rejection so find your tribe of peers, collaborators or family of artists to support you when you may need picking up from particularly difficult rejections (not all of them will hurt but some will knock you for six).

3. When you're a disabled writer, your career will not follow the same trajectory as your non-disabled peers. So don't compare your journey to anyone else's when it's not a level playing field to begin with.

4. Your health (mental and physical) should always be your priority. Don't beat yourself up when you're not able to or well enough to write (I'm still practising this). You can always come back to your writing (there's no expiry date).

5. Make taking regular breaks and resting a part of your process. Learn about your needs and demand for them to be met (I know, easier said than done).

Little Miss Burden, I hope, is about giving visibility to the historical and institutional erasure of disabled people's experiences and, let's be honest, existence in society.

When society tries to label you as just one thing or trait, it's important to write as much of you onto the page as possible. So when the dark days come (because they will) and I start to feel like I'm fading, parts of me can be found in this story. Writing this play has been difficult to say the least but incredibly rewarding to finally lay a lot of crap to rest about growing up a black, disabled woman in the UK.

Even though this play is autobiographical please feel free to explore multi-rolling and staging this story in accessible spaces/venues and inventive ways. This play is an invitation to collaborate, so the performer who plays Little Miss must be played by someone who has the lived experience of growing up with a physical impairment and/or disability. But also consider inviting and working with not only disabled performers but disabled directors, producers, set designers, production managers, sound designers, lighting designers, stage managers (trust me, they are out there!) The music mentioned in the script is suggestive rather than prescriptive.

If you're reading this, I hope the story of Little Miss Burden is a cautionary tale and a reminder of our shared humanity.

Oh and one last thing...

#SavetheNHS

Matilda Ibini, 2019

LITTLE MISS BURDEN

Little Miss Burden was first performed at the Bunker Theatre, on 4th December 2019 with the following:

CAST

LITTLE MISS	Saida Ahmed
LITTLE SIS	Ani Nelson
BIG SIS	Michelle Tiwo

CREATIVE LIST

DIRECTOR	Debbie Hannan
DESIGNER	Helen Hebert
ASSISTANT DIRECTOR	Phao May
PRODUCTION MANAGER	Pete Rickards
SOUND DESIGNER	Benjamin Grant
LIGHTING DESIGNER	Pete Rickards
SET DESIGNER	Helen Hebert
MOVEMENT DIRECTOR	Phao May
STAGE MANAGER	Ella Dixon
DRAMATURG	Jules Haworth
PRODUCER	Harts Theatre Company and Bunker Theatre

CAST

MICHELLE TIWO | BIG SIS

Michelle Tiwo is a non-binary actor, poet, poet educator and founder of Sistren podcast. Michelle's work is reflective of their identity and their communities, Nigeria & Togo via South East London.
Recent acting credits include: *Parakeet* (Boundless/Boom Shakalaka Productions); *And The Rest of Me Floats* (Bush Theatre); *Ackee and Saltfish* (BBC 3); *Faces* (dir. Joseph Adesunloye); *We Love Moses* (dir. Dionne Edwards); *The Ting* (Channel 4 Random Acts) and upcoming *Parakeet* (Boundless/Roundabout).
Other collaborations and work includes: Barbican x Boy Blue; BFI x Galdem; Eastside Education x Armed Forces Service Children; Lemonade Money Productions; The Royal College of Art, Writerz n Scribez.

ANI NELSON | LITTLE SIS

Ani trained at the Academy of Live and Recorded Arts (ALRA). Theatre credits include: *The Trick* (Bush); *Abigail's Party* (Hull Truck); *Gastronomic* (Curious Directive); *A Cratchit Christmas* (Theatre503). Screen credits include: *Roadkill* (Channel 4); *Crooked House* (Brilliant Films).

SAIDA AHMED | LITTLE MISS

Is a wheelchair using, twenty-four-year-old University Graduate. She believes that being a wheelchair user doesn't restrict her from achieving anything but encourages her to be more determined to achieve more than the average person.
Credits include: *My Favourite* (AppleCart Theatre) and working alongside Site Productions and RFL Media. Her one-woman show *Hadithi Yangu/My Story* about her disability, feminism and other people's perceptions on disability played at Camden People's Theatre.

CREATIVE

MATILDA IBINI | WRITER

Matilda Ibini is an award-winning playwright and screenwriter from London. She was awarded a scholarship from BAFTA and Warner Brothers to study a Masters in Playwriting & Screenwriting at City University and gained a Distinction. She graduated with a second upper class degree in English Literature and Creative Writing from London Metropolitan University. Her work has been shortlisted for awards such as the Soho Young Writers Award and the Alfred Fagon Award. She was part of the Royal Court Writers Program 2012/13 and was a member of Soho Theatre's Writers' Alumni Group. She was also Soho Theatre's writer-in-residence for the BBC Writersroom 10 scheme 2014/15, was Graeae Theatre's Artist-in-Residence 2017/18 and completed an attachment at the National Theatre Studio.

Her debut play *Muscovado* about slavery and the sugar trade was produced by BurntOut Theatre, premiered in October 2014 and toured the UK in 2015 starting with a run at Theatre503. *Muscovado* subsequently co-won the Alfred Fagon Audience Award 2015. She has had short plays staged at the Old Vic Theatre, Bush Theatre, Hampstead Theatre Downstairs, National Theatre Shed, St James Theatre, Royal Exchange Manchester, Birmingham Rep, Soho Theatre, Arcola Theatre, Bunker Theatre, Hackney Showroom and Vaults Festival. Matilda is currently under commission to Bush Theatre and has two film projects in development with BBC Films and a TV series in development with Wall to Wall Productions.

DEBBIE HANNAN | DIRECTOR

Debbie Hannan trained at the Royal Conservatoire of Scotland and as Trainee Director at the Royal Court. She directs new writing and makes devised theatre.

Recent credits include: *Pah-La* (Royal Court); *The Panopticon* (National Theatre of Scotland & Traverse Theatre); *Cuckoo, The Session* (Soho Theatre); *Girl Meets Boy* (developed with National Theatre of Scotland and The Yard); *Latir* (Compañia Nacional de Teatro, Mexico); *SHAME* (Bang Bang Bang Gorup); *The Wonderful World of Dissocia, The Angry Brigade* (Royal Conservatoire of Scotland); *Pandora* (Etch, Pleasance); *What We Know, Killer Joe, Conspiracy* (Royal Welsh College, the Gate); *The Five Steps, Primetime, Who Cares, Spaghetti Ocean* (Royal Court); *Lot and His God, Notes from the Underground* (Citizens Theatre); *Recreation*

(Arcola); *CauseWay, Woman of the Year* (Oran Mor); *Liberty, Equality, Fraternity* (Tron/Traverse); *Sucker* (Old Vic New Voices); *PANORAMA, Roses Are Dead* (Arches).
Credits as assistant include: *How to Hold Your Breath, Birdland, The Internet is Serious Business, God Bless the Child, The Mistress Contract* (Royal Court); *The Maids, Sleeping Beauty* (Citizens); *A Doll's House, Enquirer* (National Theatre of Scotland).
As associate, credits include: *Our Ladies of Perpetual Succour* (National Theatre of Scotland); *A Pacifist's Guide to the War on Cancer* (Complicité); *Constellations* (Royal Court - UK Tour); *Little on the Inside* (Clean Break).
As writer, credits include: *SHAME* (Bang Bang Bang Group); *Vinyl Idol* (Oran Mor); *Suffrajets* (Tron Theatre Lab).

JULES HAWORTH | DRAMATURG

JulesHaworth is Education Producer at Soho Theatre and looks after Soho's Writers' Lab, Comedy Lab, Cabaret & Drag Lab and outreach programmes for artists. Jules is part of Soho Theatre's Artistic team, considering and developing new work for the stages. She has read for playwriting competitions including the Verity Bargate Award, Tony Craze Award and Muslim Writers' Award. Jules has run playwriting workshops and talks for emerging artists with Soho Theatre, Talawa Theatre, Rich Mix, LGBTQ+ Arts, Sour Lemons, Gendered Intelligence, Traverse Theatre, Live Theatre, Somerset House and in schools and colleges in London.
As a dramaturg, Jules has worked on shows including: *Brute* by Izzy Tennyson (Ideas Tap Underbelly Award 2015, Underbelly); *Muscovado* by Matilda Ibini (Alfred Fagon Award 2015, Theatre 503); *Villain* by Martin Murphy (Offie Nominated 2018, Kings Head Theatre); *On the Edge of Me* by Yolanda Mercy (Soho Theatre and Tour); *Quarter Life Crisis* by Yolanda Mercy (Soho Theatre and Tour); *Wonderboy* by Ross Willis (Bristol Old Vic); *Dust* by Milly Thomas (Whatsonstage nominated 2019, Trafalgar Studios) and *Algorithms* by Sadie Clark (Pleasance).
Jules has also appeared as a panellist for Sphinx Theatre's *Women Centre Stage, The Listening Project* for BBC Radio 4 and as a judge for Funny Women Awards and Directors Cut.
Her play *Pigeon Steps* was longlisted for the Adrian Pagan Award 2014.

PHAO MAY | ASSISTANT DIRECTOR

Phao May trained in Acting at RADA and has since gone on to pursue a career in direction and movement. This year she worked as an assistant director for a year long programme for National Youth Theatre and is now an Associate Artist for them. Recent credits include 'Summerfest' at The Bunker, written by Yolanda Mercy, directed by Lakesha Arie-Angelo and 'Genesis' by Miller & Salmon at The Soho Theatre.

PETE RICKARDS | PRODUCTION MANAGER and LIGHTING DESIGNER

Pete Rickards is a Production Manager and Lighting Designer. His professional experience has seen him not only working in London but around the world, touring with Theatre and Music as well as working on large scale and immersive events. He has production management and tour management experience throughout Europe and the UK including Thorpe Park, and consulting for The Taussauds Group for an attraction in San Francisco. His lighting designs have been showcased in the UK, Germany and Ireland, and will soon be touring to Australia and the USA. He has designed for Sh!t Theatre, Thorpe Park, La John Joseph, The Outbound Project in the past, at venues such as Schaubüne, Soho Theatre, Lattitude Festival and Battersea Arts Centre.

BENJAMIN GRANT | SOUND DESIGNER

Benjamin Grant studied at Central School of Speech and Drama and has experience designing for Theatre, Dance and Installation, specialising in devised work and new writing. Recent sound design credits include: *Maggot Moon* (Unicorn Theatre); *I'll Take You To Mrs Cole* (Pleasance Beyond); *The Last of the Pelican Daughters* (Pleasance Beyond); *Education Education Education* (Trafalgar Studios); *The War of The Worlds* (New Diorama Theatre); *Prurience* (Southbank Centre/Guggenheim Museum NYC); *The Road Awaits Us* (Sadler's Wells) and other credits include: Associate Sound Designer for *Beware of Pity* (Schaubühne) and Associate Sound Designer for *The Kid Stays In The Picture* (Royal Court). Benjamin is an Associate Artist of The Wardrobe Ensemble.

HELEN HEBERT | SET DESIGNER

Helen Hebert is a set designer based in London. She trained at Royal Central School of Speech and Drama graduating with First Class Honours. Her work focuses on performance design and installations.

She has worked as an assistant designer in the design studio Curious Space creating immersive spaces for museums, galleries, public spaces and performance.

The creative team of her last project *Sh*t Happens* received an Offie nomination for Best Show in the short run category. Recent Credits: *Little Miss Burden* (The Bunker); *Shit Happens* (Camden People Theatre – Offie nomination); *The Decline of a Distant Memory* (RADA); T*he Way of the World Suffragette City* (assistant designer)

ELLA DIXON | STAGE MANAGER

Ella Dixon has worked as a technical stage manager on a wide range of projects. Last year touring the UK with one man show *Love, Bombs and Apples* (2018 UK tour) and Soho Theatre's *Half Breed* (2018 UK tour). When not on the road, Ella works as a more traditional stage manager in a variety of London venues, last year working with Jessie Cave on *Sunrise* and award winning comedian Natalie Palamedie's new show *Nate* (2018 Soho theatre) which also received a run at the Edinburgh fringe festival. Ella has just returned to London from nine months in Australia, working at as venue manager at the Adelaide Fringe, as well as stage manager at one of Sydney's best independent venues The Hayes Theatre. Ella is thrilled to be working on *Little Miss Burden*.

HARTS THEATRE COMPANY

Harts Theatre Company founded by Artistic Director, Ann Akin, in 2013 aims to produce entertaining and inspiring artistic work with outstanding artists in London.

From its inception we have also produced high quality opportunities with young and emerging talent that pushes the boundaries to shine a spotlight on unearthed talent in different areas of London.

We produce two annual festival; Young Harts Writing Festival, which has a strong vision to break down boundaries by merging the worlds of young creatives with the professional industry and Sound Of Mind, an audio and visual arts mental wellbeing festival. We are committed to developing the arts community: developing young performers and artists in their chosen fields through professional training and support.

BUNKER THEATRE

The Bunker believes in artists. We give ambitious artists a home in which to share their work with adventurous audiences. We are champions of each company that we programme, and we want to ensure our stage is filled with exhilarating and contemporary theatre featuring artists that represent the world that we live in.
The Bunker was opened in October 2016 by founding directors Joshua McTaggart and Joel Fisher. The theatre's first year of work included the award-winning sell-out show *Skin A Cat*, Cardboard Citizen's 25th Anniversary epic *Home Truths*, and the world premiere of *31 Hours*. In-house productions have included *Abigail*, *Eyes Closed*, *Ears Covered* and *Devil With The Blue Dress*.
In September 2018, Artistic Director Chris Sonnex joined Executive Director David Ralf to lead the theatre's small, dedicated team, several of whom were involved in the original conversion of an underground car park into The Bunker space. Bunker Theatre Productions CIC is a not-for-profit theatre, which currently receives no public subsidy.

ACKNOWLEDGEMENTS

Little Miss Burden is definitely without a doubt the product of a community of supporters and loved ones. I have so much love and respect for my support network both professionally and personally who enabled and believed in me to tell this story.

First thanks goes to my family: Mummy, Big Sis, Lil' Sis and Lil' Bro

Soho Writers' Alumni Group of 2013–2018 (special big ups to Amelia Sutherland, Natasha Sutton-Williams, Tom Powell, Phoebe Eclair-Powell, Iskandar Sharazuddin, Amy Bethan-Evans and Ross Willis).

p.s. Amelia Sutherland (is an AMAZING reader and dramaturg – hire her!)

Huge thanks and love to everyone who read drafts and helped with readings and supported me at different stages throughout this process.

Bryony Kimmings, Jules Haworth, Stewart Pringle, Deirdre O'Halloran, Arts Council England, Madani Younis, Omar Elerian, Vilma Jackson, Jacqui Adeniji-Williams, Lilly Burton, Tom Parkinson, Robert Bertrand, Nicole Latchana, Carol Ellis, Oladipo Agboluaje, Ola Animashawun, Gabriel Bisset-Smith, Jen Tan, Amelia Stubberfield, Rebecca Yeo, Gabriella Schmidt, Sarah Stevens, Sarah Baiden, Melanie Rendall, Liz, Alice and Rhys.

My secondary school teacher Mrs Gallagher for whom I may not have ever embarked on this wild journey, were it not for her gentle encouragement

Thank you to the incredibly supportive theatre companies: Graeae Theatre Company, Tamasha Theatre Company and Talawa Theatre Company.

Isobel Mascarenhas-Whitman and Alex Tennyson at Type One (Creative Technology) for their brilliant projections and captioning during the very first initial R&D for Little Miss Burden.

Bryony Kimmings Summer Workshop Group of July 2016: Beth, Victoria, Pippa, Michelle, Sarah, Lisa, Imogen, Gareth,

Marina, Ellie, Melissa, Kate (you are all incredibly generous and supportive artists).

My wonderful champion and agent Ikenna Obiekwe.

To the incredibly kind and uber talented cast: Michelle Tiwo, Saida Ahmed & Ani Nelson

All the lovely and generous team at the Bunker Theatre and the brilliant creative team behind the production: Phao, Ella, Pete, Ben, Helen, Holly, Hannah, Ed – thank you all so much for your hard work and belief in the story. (Big ups to Gabriel Ajala for the wicked poster!)

Big love and thanks to Chris Sonnex and David Ralf for their unwavering support and kindness. Long live the Bunker!

Debbie Hannan – a directing don and generous collaborator.

Harts Theatre Company – headed by Ann Akin – a phenomenal woman of indomitable spirit.

My Avengers a.k.a team of carers: Christine, Alice, Kate, Georgina, Rebecca, Jean, Anya, Mona, Emma and Ola.

I could probably fill all these pages with more names of people to thank but I'll end here and say thank you to the rest of you in the next one.

"There's really no such thing as the 'voiceless'. There are only the deliberately silenced, or the preferably unheard." – Arundhati Roy

For Mummy, Ayo, Jide, Tolu, Grandma and Adebayo

CHARACTERS

BIG SIS – *female, black, eldest sibling*
LITTLE MISS (L.M) – *female, black, physical impairment or wheelchair user, middle sibling*
LIL' SIS – *female, black, youngest sibling*

Suggestions for multi-rolling

BIG SIS *plays* DOCTOR/HERBALIST/PASTOR/CJ/JEN/CONTROL/F1/JESSIE/GRANDMA/TEACHER/FADE
LIL' SIS *plays* MUM/INTERPRETER/NURSE/SELIN/JANE/F2/JOSIE/ETTY/JEAN
LITTLE MISS *plays* LGMD

A suggestion for performers:
All wear denim dungarees in the spirit of the nineties era.
BIG SIS *wears a red T-shirt.*
LITTLE MISS *wears a yellow T-shirt.*
LIL' SIS *wears a green T-shirt.*

PROLOGUE

Present day in an accessible space.

This is a welcoming space. Who you are and where you are from or how you got here is irrelevant. What is important is that you are here or you are reading this and that's what matters.

LIL' SIS *places a large book on top of an empty stool in the centre of the spotlight.*

BIG SIS *wearing a colourful jumper like those 90's children's TV presenters (you know the ones, with their sleeves rolled up to the elbow and an optimism beaming from the jumper). She picks up a thick, colourful, tattered storybook. On the cover it reads Little Miss Burden. She perches on the stool.*

BIG SIS Shall we have a look at what book is in today's story corner?

Waits for audience's response.

LIL' SIS We can't hear you.

Waits for audience's response.

BIG SIS *responds to audience's response.*

BIG SIS That's more like it. Today we're going to read the story of Little Miss Burden.

LIL' SIS Oooooooooooooooooooooo.

BIG SIS Little Miss Burden was born with her right foot on her left and her left foot on her right, which made walking in a straight line oh so confusing.

Her arms were the shape of bows but she couldn't shoot arrows.

LIL' SIS *chuckles like a child in on the joke, think drunken-woodpecker type laugh.*

LIL' SIS Because they're her arms.

BIG SIS Exactly but she could shoot dirty looks because that's how you survived the mean streets of Hackney in the nineties.

BIG SIS *hands the book to* **LIL' SIS.**

LIL' SIS Yes. My turn. Little Miss Burden worked as the spokesperson for all disabled people in the whole wide world –

BIG SIS – and whole wide galaxies –

LIL' SIS – and whole wide universes –

BIG SIS – in any and all alternate realities –

LIL' SIS – in all time continuums till kingdom come.

BIG SIS Every disabled person?

LIL' SIS Yes. Every. Single. One. She won her title by a landslide of votes, beating her rival Little Miss Busy-Body, or as she likes to call her Little Miss Bitchy-Body. Booooooo – we don't like Little Miss Bitchy-Body.

LIL' SIS/BIG SIS Booooooo!

LIL' SIS *hands the book back to* **BIG SIS.**

BIG SIS Little Miss Burden lived behind a menstrual red door in a cold, miserable, frowny place called London. But a famous celebrity lived a few doors down from her. Anyone care to take a guess. I bet you won't –

LIL' SIS – Spice Girls? –

BIG SIS – no but –

LIL' SIS – Dale Winton? –

BIG SIS – no –

LIL' SIS – I've got it! Cilla Black –

BIG SIS – it was Mr Bean! Mr Bean.

LIL' SIS *makes a shocked face. We think she is disappointed, it is in fact the face of an excited child who's just been told the best secret in the world.*

For legality, I should mention it wasn't in fact the actor Rowan Atkinson but merely a Poundland version all the children on her street called Mr Bean, but she doesn't need to know that.

In her excitement **LIL' SIS** *snatches the book from* **BIG SIS**'*s clutches.*

LIL' SIS Right. Little Miss Burden lived with her family because she didn't believe in paying bills like council tax. What's council tax?

BIG SIS It's basically a monthly fine for existing on a planet that we didn't ask to be put on.

LIL' SIS *slams book shut.*

What?

LIL' SIS You didn't think we were going to tell Little Miss Burden's story without her.

BIG SIS This isn't Hollywood –

LIL' SIS – or the West End –

BIG SIS – or most fringe venues.

L.M Shade!

They high five.

BIG SIS In this pocket of time and space–

L.M – we trust people to tell their own stories.

The book is yanked out of **BIG SIS**'*s hands by an unseen force and sucked under a door.*

LIL' SIS But trust us – we didn't plan that.

The performer playing **BIG SIS** *introduces themselves and describes their appearance and gives an embarrassing detail about themselves (doesn't have to be related to their appearance or too personal). And all the characters they will be playing.*

BIG SIS And as Big Sis it means I'm charge of everyone and everything.

The performer playing **LIL' SIS** *introduces themselves and describes their appearance and gives an embarrassing detail about themselves (doesn't have to be related to their appearance or too personal). And all the characters they will be playing.*

LIL' SIS And as Lil' Sis I'm in charge of all you youngsters. If you're ninety or less, you're a youngster.

The performer playing **LITTLE MISS** *introduces themselves and describes their appearance and gives an embarrassing detail about themselves (doesn't have to be related to heir appearance or too personal). And all the characters they will be playing.*

L.M And as Little Miss, I'm in charge of informing everyone that this show is taking a laid-back approach. Meaning you don't need our permission to move, make noise, sing along, leave, take a break from the show and feel welcome to return at any point. Latecomers always welcomed never turfed.

BIG SIS The only thing we do ask.

LIL' SIS Is that mobile phones are on silent.

L.M Yes and that you enjoy the show, in whatever way that feels comfortable to you. So we're going back in time but as I don't have a Tardis, you're going to imagine that I could still walk.

BIG SIS Let's do this.

WORLD 1 – BIRTH CANAL

The sound of a song in the style of En Vogue – ***"FREE YOUR MIND"***[1] *floods the stage as* **BIG SIS, LITTLE MISS** *and* **LIL' SIS** *take their starting positions. They do a very practiced choreography.* **LIL' SIS** *looks to* **BIG SIS** *when she forgets a move. When they finish they strike a pose.*

Music abruptly stops.

BIG SIS We are the coolest –

L.M – living –

BIG SIS – coolest, living, fiercest –

LIL' SIS – coolest, living, fiercest, super talented –

L.M – girl band history's ever assembled.

BIG SIS We're bigger than the Spice Girls, All Saints, B*Witched and S Club 7 put together –

L.M – you've probably heard of us –

LIL' SIS *(mutters)* We haven't come up with a name yet?

BIG SIS Don't tell them that! Or they won't think we're legit.

---

1 A license to produce LITTLE MISS BURDEN does not include a performance license for "Free Your Mind" The publisher and author suggest that the licensee contact PRS to ascertain the music publisher and contact such music publisher to license or acquire permission for performance of the song. If a license or permission is unattainable for "Free Your Mind", the licensee may not use the song in LITTLE MISS BURDEN but should create an original composition in a similar style or use a similar song in the public domain. For further information, please see Music Use Note on page iii.

BIG SIS *looks away embarrassed. She has to change the subject.*

We know why you're here.

LIL' SIS 'Cos you bought tickets.

L.M And you want a show. But not just any show.

BIG SIS You definitely wouldn't have seen this one before. Ok so, let me set the scene. It's the autumn of nineteen ninety-one, and I'm an intelligent, gorgeously dark skinned, five-year-old girl about to have her perfect life with Mum disrupted by –

LIL' SIS – and I'm not here yet. I don't arrive till ninety-five. The blessing Mum was really waiting for.

BIG SIS *and* **LITTLE MISS** *roll their eyes.*

BIG SIS Right, it's eight a.m. and we're at Homerton hospital, East London.

LIL' SIS The midwife is readying herself to deliver her two hundred and forty fifth-baby. She assures Mum that her body is doing exactly what it's meant to.

LIL' SIS *hyperventilates as if in labour, she makes exaggerated expressions of pain on her face.*

BIG SIS Trust it to push, remind it to breathe. You can do this.

BIG SIS *begins hyperventilating.*

Mum's this calm twenty-nine-year-old Nigerian.

LIL' SIS This wasn't the first time she'd evicted tenants from her body.

BIG SIS That's Mum you're talking about like some corrupt landlord.

LIL' SIS I'm just trying to make it interesting. It's boring the way you tell it.

BIG SIS Stick to the facts.

LIL' SIS *(mimicking)* Stick to the facts.

BIG SIS *(trying to get the story back on track)* The smiling, inquisitive faces of the student doctors trying to suppress their uneasiness as Mum delivered this wriggling, ticking sack of blood, hair and fluids. A nurse dabs the build-up of sweat across the midwife's brow as she uses pliers to cut the cord and defuse the bomb of cries from this bouncing baby girl.

BIG SIS *cradles her arms pretending to carry a baby and passes it to* **LIL' SIS**, *who pretends to drop the baby.*

LITTLE MISS *is born, like a pageant winner winning first prize. She whips out a bouquet of flowers and crowns herself.*

L.M Isn't she lovely?

Isn't she wonderful?

Isn't she precious?

Less than one minute old.

Mum sung to me as I was handed to her.

LIL' SIS See. She's not sticking to the facts! And she was there.

BIG SIS You're doing too Much.

L.M Fine. I was –

LIL' SIS – carefully handed to mum –

L.M – that's not exactly how I remember it.

BIG SIS And how do you remember it? Enlighten us.

L.M I came shooting out of Mum like a bullet. Taking out a doctor, the nurses and four of the six student doctors. No time to lose, I shake off the gunk and bits off my body, chew through the umbilical cord and tell Mum laters. I had a date with the mandem. Mum stops me in my tracks, begging for a cuddle. I look at her outstretched arms and something in me can't resist. I nestle into her warm chest and listen to the hypnotic beat of her heart.

The sound of two heartbeats beating out of sync like they are communicating. The two heartbeats merge into one funky rhythmic beat of...

A song plays in the style of Cleopatra ***"COMIN' ATCHA"***[1] *plays.*

The **THREE SISTERS** *dance to the song.*

Music lowers but the melody plays under the next scene.

---

1 A license to produce LITTLE MISS BURDEN does not include a performance license for "Comin' Atcha" The publisher and author suggest that the licensee contact PRS to ascertain the music publisher and contact such music publisher to license or acquire permission for performance of the song. If a license or permission is unattainable for "Comin' Atcha", the licensee may not use the song in LITTLE MISS BURDEN but should create an original composition in a similar style or use a similar song in the public domain. For further information, please see Music Use Note on page iii.

WORLD 2 – WOMB 2.0

BIG SIS, LIL' SIS *and* **LITTLE MISS** *deliver their lines with more energy than a music video, it's like they are bursting to get the story out before it explodes inside of them. Think children fizzing on sherbet and cola whilst trying to act "cool".*

BIG SIS Stamford Hill-

LIL' SIS Council house number four-

L.M Age five-

BIG SIS We lived with Mum at nineteen Cylinder Road-

LIL' SIS In a slender two bed, terraced house between a Chinese family and a Jamaican family.

L.M Behind the liquorice red front door was a living room, a kitchen, garden and guest room which was haunted.

LIL' SIS It was, always cold.

BIG SIS That's because it was the only room in the house without central heating. Up a flight of stairs was the bathroom, my bedroom that I shared with Little Miss.

LIL' SIS And then my room that I shared with Mum –

L.M – shared?

LIL' SIS Fine. I slept in her bed.

L.M Anyway our house was infested –

LGMD – Boo.

L.M Who said that? Did you not hear that?

LIL' SIS Hear what?

BIG SIS That's not the line...

LIL' SIS Just give her a moment. Our house was infested with...

L.M ...rats, snails and slugs. This is where rats came to die, fed up of life on the streets, in the shadows, hiding from stray cats and preying foxes –

BIG SIS – alright, alright Attenborough. I think they get it.

L.M Snails and slugs slipped in from the jungle that was our garden and left tracks all over the kitchen, like dried glue.

BIG SIS Our house wasn't by any means perfect –

LIL' SIS – or even pretty –

BIG SIS – but it was a home.

L.M Full of delicious smells of jollof rice, pounded yam and egusi, fried plantain and egg –

All three do a chef's kiss.

LIL' SIS Fried plan-tain.

BIG SIS Like Olu Main-tain.

L.M Mum's the secret ingredient in everything she makes.

LIL' SIS Lazy lie-in Saturdays, fights, spats, tears, songs, birthdays –

L.M – fire brigade when I accidentally blew up the microwave –

BIG SIS – calling the police round to pretend we were in *The Bill* –

L.M – Christmas days –

BIG SIS – the Christmas without electricity –

L.M – Easter egg hunts –

LIL' SIS – the morning rat caught in the trap –

L.M – New Year's Resolutions –

BIG SIS – wearing winter clothes around the house so we didn't have to turn on the heating –

L.M – and lots and lots of warmth and love. We were passionate about making Mum proud.

They salute to **MUM**.

LGMD *(First speaks)* Some facts you should know about Mum.

LIL' SIS Mum came to the UK in the summer of nineteen ninety –

BIG SIS – with my then four-year-old butt.

L.M Before I descended from heaven.

LIL' SIS *(laughs a little too hard)* More like saved the best till last. Me!

BIG SIS Well not exactly last, three years after the *(coughs)* the hiccup –

LIL' SIS – you're not even trying to be subtle –

BIG SIS – our Lil' Bro was born –

L.M – AKA Mr Okele –

BIG SIS – but his narrative kinda disrupts our dynamic –

LIL' SIS – our flow –

BIG SIS – exactly! Our flow and we won't pass the Bechdel test if we talk about him any longer.

LIL' SIS Sorry bro. Nuff love though.

BIG SIS *and* **LITTLE MISS** *roll their eyes.*

L.M Mum was the second oldest – like moi – of six siblings. We have a lot in common. She was really close with her dad who died on her twenty ninth birthday – so celebrating is often bittersweet for her.

BIG SIS Mum's always been very spiritual. With her Yoruba tongue, Muslim name and Christian heart, she has exercised endless patience and love to helping others.

LIL' SIS She has the best hair. We have lots more in common.

BIG SIS Mum's a creative soul, loves music, parties, would braid and style all our hair in different styles and colours because we could never afford to go to a salon.

LIL' SIS The top five styles Mum could braid.

Chart countdown music plays. [1]

L.M In at number five.

LIL' SIS *Ko l'ese*

BIG SIS No legs.

LIL' SIS Braids that go straight from the front to the back like a race track. Great for sewing in weaves or wearing wigs. The reverse of this is called *Ipako elede.*

BIG SIS Pigs head. Don't ask.

L.M In at number four.

BIG SIS *Suku.*

LIL' SIS Closely weaved gourd.

BIG SIS Braids weaved like the mouth of a bottle. Can be decorated with coloured beads or cowrie shells.

L.M Making a surprise entry at number three.

LIL' SIS *Pa nu mo.*

BIG SIS Closed mouth.

LIL' SIS Braids that start in the front and back that meet in the middle. Not to be confused with *suku*. Think the way, the mouth of a Venus fly trap opens and closes. *(Goes to touch* **LITTLE MISS**'*s hair)* Oh my God. I love your – ow – your hair just bit me.

---

1 A license to produce LITTLE MISS BURDEN does not include a performance license for any third-party or copyrighted music. Licensees should create an original composition or use music in the public domain. For further information, please see Music Use Note on page iii.

L.M She does that when people don't get my permission first... Didn't quite make it to number one this time but a childhood favourite at number two.

BIG SIS *Suku ologede*

LIL' SIS Closely weaved like a banana.

BIG SIS The more extravagant sibling of the *suku* except braids aren't straight, they are curved like a banana with a tight bun on top. Really accentuates one's egg-shaped head.

L.M Not surprisingly, in at number one, as seen on Beyoncé, Brandy, Alicia Keys and Cleopatra. Drum roll please.

*The opening beats of a song in the style of Magic System **"PREMIER GAOU"**[1] plays. Then abruptly cuts out.*

LIL' SIS *Biba.*

BIG SIS Single plaits.

LIL' SIS The versatile single plait, the box braid, the pick and drop, twist, micro braids, Ghana braids. Mum's hands weaved magic in our hair.

L.M Mum's also our stylist.

LIL' SIS And a style icon.

BIG SIS Mum couldn't afford to dress her world famous girl band on a single salary...of several part-time jobs.

LIL' SIS So we'd go with her to Dalston market and pick out fabrics we liked the colour of –

---

1 A license to produce LITTLE MISS BURDEN does not include a performance license for "Premier Gaou" The publisher and author suggest that the licensee contact PRS to ascertain the music publisher and contact such music publisher to license or acquire permission for performance of the song. If a license or permission is unattainable for "Premier Gaou", the licensee may not use the song in LITTLE MISS BURDEN but should create an original composition in a similar style or use a similar song in the public domain. For further information, please see Music Use Note on page iii.

L.M – and she'd sew us new outfits for any occasion –

BIG SIS – birthdays, school discos, church anniversaries, Christmas, sold-out concerts –

LIL' SIS An unsung fashion designer to this day.

L.M Shame none of us inherited her wicked fashion sense.

LIL' SIS Speak for yourself.

BIG SIS Yeah. We don't dress like a rainbow vomited on us.

LIL' SIS *chuckles and high fives* **BIG SIS.**

L.M Anyway Mum won the Guinness World Record for biggest heart in the universe. Worked in McDonalds, as a school dinner lady, care homes, domestic violence organisation and sheltered housing. It's in her DNA.

LIL' SIS Always serving others any chance she got.

L.M Anytime we were upset about anything, Mum would embrace us in her comforting arms and sing:

A song plays in the style of Bob Marley's – ***"THREE LITTLE BIRDS"***[2] .

LGMD It won't.

LITTLE MISS *looks around worried and misses her cue to salute with her* **SISTERS.**

An alarm rings loudly.

---

2 A license to produce LITTLE MISS BURDEN does not include a performance license for "Three Little Birds" The publisher and author suggest that the licensee contact PRS to ascertain the music publisher and contact such music publisher to license or acquire permission for performance of the song. If a license or permission is unattainable for "Three Little Birds", the licensee may not use the song in LITTLE MISS BURDEN but should create an original composition in a similar style or use a similar song in the public domain. For further information, please see Music Use Note on page iii.

L.M What's going on? We didn't rehearse this.

LIL' SIS We interrupt the scheduled show for breaking news.

BIG SIS A mysterious grey door has appeared on the outskirts of the Story Sanctuary.

LIL' SIS No one knows the origins of this door, but the public is being warned to keep a wider than wide berth.

BIG SIS The door which does in fact have a handle as incorrectly reported earlier, seems to defy the laws of gravity and door craftsmanship. It stands on its own and one can seemingly walk around it, so where it leads to is unknowable.

LIL' SIS There have been several attempts to open the door and even dismantle it, but all attempts have failed. It seems the material the door is made from is impenetrable and the door is solidly locked. Tourists are discouraged from taking selfies with the door.

BIG SIS Witnesses report hearing a low whistle emanating from the door, but official reports debunk this.

LIL' SIS *and* **BIG SIS** *point at the door.*

In the event of an emergency, no one is permitted to open that door, particularly you Little Miss.

L.M Why? What's the doors deal?

LIL' SIS Under no circumstance must it ever be opened. Some doors just shouldn't be doors.

BIG SIS Don't think about the door.

LIL' SIS Don't look at the door.

BIG SIS Don't draw attention to the door.

LIL' SIS Sometimes doors keep danger out –

BIG SIS – and other times doors keep danger in –

LIL' SIS – and sometimes doors themselves –

BIG SIS/LIL' SIS – are the danger.

L.M Don't say it like that.

LITTLE MISS *trying not to scratch her itch of curiosity.*

LIL' SIS As far as we're concerned, that door doesn't exist. *(As* **MUM***)* You have to promise me, no matter whoever it is, even if they say they know me. You must never open this door for anyone.

L.M It's just a door.

BIG SIS No matter how hard things get. You won't be tempted to even touch its handle.

L.M You can't be serious –

BIG SIS/LIL' SIS Promise us!

L.M Ok-ok, I promise. Can we continue now?

BIG SIS The scheduled story will now resume shortly.

Long TV beep.

WORLD 3 – PLAYGROUND JUNGLE

School bell rings.

The laughter of children playing in a primary school playground. **LITTLE MISS** *is sat with her friends* **F1** *and* **F2.**

BIG SIS Primary school–

LIL' SIS School gates–

L.M Age nine-and-a-half–

BIG SIS The three pillars that held up Little Miss's life were school, hospitals, and church.

L.M School was by far my favourite.

LIL' SIS You were Little Miss Popular back then.

L.M I don't like to brag. I had a particular pasttime for anyone who'd listen.

BIG SIS An unlikely storyteller was developing her skills shall we say.

LIL' SIS To all the kids whose parents didn't sign their permission slip so they couldn't be taught Sex Ed in primary school. This one's for you.

F1 Soooo. What did you see? What did the video show?

F2 What exactly is *(whispers)* S-E-X?

L.M Well, when a man and a woman love each other. They take off all their clothes, turn invisible and run around a bed. The man chases the woman, but sometimes the woman can chase the man, if he's short.

The woman runs around so fast that she trips on the corner of the bed and falls onto her back. Women always fall onto their backs.

F2 Onto the bed?

L.M Yeah. I'm gonna practise it when I get home.

F1 Then what happened?

L.M Then the man continues running, he runs around and around until he's tired but the woman is taking up all the space on the bed, so he falls on top of her. Because they've both been running so much they're really sweaty and so they're sliding and wriggling on each other. Then the man's *(Whispers)* willy turns pink.

F1 It's so ugly.

F2 I've seen one in real life. My baby brothers's when my mum was bathing him. His is cute though.

L.M Anyway the man is wriggling and then he slides it inside the woman's...pink hole. They're still hot and sweaty and in order to cool down they keep wiggling and sliding on each other. But it's not working. The man's the first to get tired. Men are always the first to get tired. He stretches his arms out and he does this big loud yawn and then... *(Mumbles)* Something comes out.

F1 What?

L.M *(whispers)* Something comes out of his willy.

F2 What comes out? Wee-wee?

L.M No, it's different. I don't know. It looks like...remember at the school fête when you ate that whole bag of candy floss by yourself, and then you drank that whole can of Sprite and then you threw up.

F1 Yeah.

L.M It looks like that but not pink.

F2 Ewwwww.

F1 Into the woman's...

F2 Pink hole?

F1 Don't say that.

F2 Sex is disgusting. Is it even legal?

F1 *(gasps)* I can't believe you said it. Well my mum told me you can only have *sex* if you have a marriage certificate.

L.M I never want to get married.

F1 becomes **TEACHER** *and* **F2** *becomes* **MUM. LITTLE MISS** *continues chatting with her friends.*

TEACHER *(to* **MUM***)* She's very bright.

MUM Thank you.

TEACHER She's been falling down a lot more lately. We've had to tell her to stop running. It's becoming quite challenging on our staff.

MUM Right. She's not said anything –

TEACHER – we have to put out a chair for her in assembly because she can't get off the floor without support. We can't have teachers picking her up like a baby.

L.M I'm not sure how they make babies.

MUM She's fine, there's nothing wrong with her. You said so yourself, she's a bright girl.

L.M Umm, I think you can just take one you like from the hospital.

TEACHER Yes she is, but we don't want her brightness dimming and thus becoming a problem for her teachers.

MUM She's not a problem.

TEACHER I know that, sorry I just mean that we are doing everything we can but her – the situation doesn't seem to be improving.

MUM We are still waiting for the results from some tests she's had.

TEACHER Well as soon as you know, please let us know and we can move forward from there.

MUM Yes, of course.

TEACHER *leaves.* **LITTLE MISS** *looks up and spots* **MUM**, *she rushes over and takes* **MUM**'*s hand.*

So what did you learn at school today?

L.M Mum have you ever turned invisible?

Video game warp sound effect.[1]

We're hurtling down her imagination highway, through galaxies, defying space, time and most importantly gravity. We are voyaging where few have ventured – we're heading towards endless landscapes primed for adventures handily nicknamed 'The Sanctuary'.

---

1 A license to produce LITTLE MISS BURDEN does not include a performance license for any third-party or copyrighted sound effects. Licensees should create their own.

WORLD 4 – BETTEROBICS

BIG SIS Clinic–

L.M *(sad)* Physios–

LIL' SIS Age ten and a few days... Is that where you and Mum went after school on Thursdays?

LITTLE MISS *nods.*

JESSIE Hi Little Miss.

JOSIE Remember us?

L.M ...Jessie? ...Josie?

JOSIE I'm Josie.

JESSIE And I'm Jessie. Confusing right?

LGMD I hate Mary-Kate and Ashley.

L.M Sorry, what did you say?

JESSIE Have you been practising your exercise daily?

JOSIE You know you'll only get better with practice.

L.M Yes.

JESSIE Are you sure?

JOSIE You wouldn't lie to us, would you?

LGMD They calling you a liar.

L.M I do them every morning, when I get back from school and before I go to bed.

JESSIE You do want to get better, don't you?

LGMD Better? What does she think better looks like?

L.M Yeah course.

JOSIE You want to make it easier for Mum, right?

L.M Course.

JOSIE I know it hurts.

LGMD Try all you want – you're not going to get rid of me that easily.

L.M How long will I need to keep doing this till?

JESSIE Till you're all better.

JOSIE But only if you keep doing them without fail.

LGMD If it worked they'd call it physi-yes.

JESSIE So go on.

JOSIE Give it a try.

JESSIE Try it, it'll help.

LGMD *(mocking)* Try it. It'll help.

JOSIE Go on, you have to keep trying.

JESSIE Keep trying.

JOSIE Keep going.

LGMD This is so stupid.

L.M I know.

JESSIE Try it again.

JOSIE Come on. Try harder.

LGMD Ouch.

JESSIE Why aren't you trying?

L.M *(breathless)* I am...

JOSIE Well it doesn't look like you are.

L.M It's not me.

JESSIE What do you mean?

L.M I don't know why it's not working.

JOSIE Maybe you're not doing it right?

LGMD Maybe you're not right?

JESSIE Are you sure you're doing them every day?

L.M Mum sends me to my room and won't let me watch Sailor Moon if I don't.

JESSIE These are not the results of someone who practices every day.

JOSIE When do you do them?

JESSIE Who's watching you?

JOSIE I know they're hard.

JESSIE It's ok if you haven't been doing them.

JOSIE We'll understand.

L.M I'm not lying.

JOSIE You've been doing these for a while now.

JESSIE We should have seen some improvement by now.

L.M I'm feeling better.

LGMD Nothing's changed.

L.M I have more energy.

LGMD *(yawns)* I'm so sleepy.

JESSIE Maybe these aren't the right ones,

JOSIE That could be why they haven't been working for her?

L.M Yeah...maybe...

LITTLE MISS *closes her eyes, fatigued and breathless, she's been pushing herself, past her limits.*

Video game warp sound effect.[1]

---

1 A license to produce LITTLE MISS BURDEN does not include a performance license for any third-party or copyrighted sound effects. Licensees should create their own.

WORLD 5 – DIAGNO-SEAS ISLAND

BIG SIS *and* **LIL' SIS** *sit in front of* **LITTLE MISS** *like an isosceles triangle, that's all the maths you're getting in this script.*

BIG SIS Hammersmith hospital–

LIL' SIS A labyrinth–

L.M Age ten and a half–

DOCTOR Mrs-Mrs Abra-ca-dabra?

L.M Mum?

MUM It's Miss.

DOCTOR Mrs A, we're not quite sure what's wrong with her. Do you have any family history of any recurring illnesses?

MUM *shakes her head.*

Are you sure?

MUM *nods.*

We could perform some genetic tests to see where it could have come from?

BIG SIS *and* **LIL' SIS** *stand up and break out of character for a moment.*

LIL' SIS There's a saying –

BIG SIS – it's just not this one –

LIL' SIS – can you just let me –

BIG SIS – fine but you just can't make up sayings and claim that everyone says them –

LIL' SIS – when a Nigerian woman cries there's a flood on the other side of the world.

L.M We're not blaming black women for natural disasters.

BIG SIS Or climate change.

LIL' SIS You've got to remember, Mum's Nigerian first and a mother second. And Nigerian women don't cry.

BIG SIS Ever!

LIL' SIS Ever?

The sound of a record scratching.

BIG SIS *and* **LIL' SIS** *dance to a song in the style of Outkast* ***"MS. JACKSON"***[1].

Record scratches out.

L.M They do cry. Mum's just never cried in front of you two.

BIG SIS *and* **LIL' SIS** *sit back down into their characters.*

DOCTOR *hands* **MUM** *a tissue. She wipes her face.*

DOCTOR Or if there is a possible relation between you and your partner that could also explain this abnormality.

MUM ...Are you – are you asking if my husband is also my brother?

DOCTOR Well no, I'm just stating genetically, mutations can occur if the parents are –

---

1 A license to produce LITTLE MISS BURDEN does not include a performance license for "Ms. Jackson" The publisher and author suggest that the licensee contact PRS to ascertain the music publisher and contact such music publisher to license or acquire permission for performance of the song. If a license or permission is unattainable for "Ms. Jackson", the licensee may not use the song in LITTLE MISS BURDEN but should create an original composition in a similar style or use a similar song in the public domain. For further information, please see Music Use Note on page iii.

MUM He's not –

L.M Hold up. I'm a mutant! Am I an X-Men?

MUM *and* **DOCTOR** *share a look.*

DOCTOR Are you sure?

MUM Yes.

DOCTOR Confident.

MUM Yes!

DOCTOR There aren't definitive cures for a lot of genetic conditions yet but that could change in the future.

MUM So what does that mean for my daughter now?

DOCTOR We can't know for sure but it's likely she'll need physical aids to help her mobilise like leg braces, crutches, a wheelchair even.

MUM Wheelchair?

DOCTOR Yes, it's a chair on wheels. We'll know what exactly she is suffering from once we've performed more tests. We're going to do everything we can, to get to the bottom of this. *(To* **LITTLE MISS***)* We don't want you getting worse and upsetting Mum now, do we?

MUM *exits the scene and enter* **NURSE** *holding a clipboard.*

DOCTOR *and* **NURSE** *perform a physical examination on* **LITTLE MISS.**

CK levels?

NURSE High.

DOCTOR Ability?

NURSE Low.

LITTLE MISS *sadly holds the word 'ability' and 'low' in her head.*

DOCTOR Mobility?

NURSE Slow.

DOCTOR Can she tie her shoes?

NURSE Pass.

DOCTOR Can she get dressed?

NURSE Pass.

DOCTOR Can feed self?

NURSE Pass.

L.M Yes –

DOCTOR – fashion sense?

NURSE Fail.

L.M But –

DOCTOR – common sense?

NURSE Fail.

L.M Hey!

DOCTOR Can roll tongue?

> **DOCTOR** *demonstrates by rolling tongue and* **LITTLE MISS** *copies.*

NURSE Pass.

DOCTOR Friends at school?

NURSE Fail.

L.M That's not –

DOCTOR Can speak up?

NURSE Fail.

DOCTOR Is a good Christian?

NURSE Fail.

DOCTOR Is a good person?

NURSE Results pending.

DOCTOR Can be a fully functioning person integrated into society?

NURSE Further tests required.

L.M *(whispers)* Further tests required... Hear that Professor X?

> **DOCTOR** *and* **NURSE** *look over their shoulder and stare* **LITTLE MISS** *down.* **LITTLE MISS** *rejects their gaze.*
>
> *Video game warp sound effect.*[1]
>
> *We're hurtling down her imagination highway, through galaxies, defying space, time and most importantly gravity. Back to The Sanctuary.*

---

1 A license to produce LITTLE MISS BURDEN does not include a performance license for any third-party or copyrighted sound effects. Licensees should create their own.

WORLD 6 – WEAKEST LINKEST

Lights up as **LITTLE MISS** *opens her eyes.*

Intense quiz show music plays.[1]

BIG SIS *puts on a pair of large red glasses and a neon orange bicycle helmet. She looks as close to Anne Robinson as a black girl can.*

BIG SIS *(to* **LIL' SIS***)* In British politics who is our current Prime Minister?

LIL' SIS Tony Blair.

BIG SIS Correct.

LIL' SIS Bank.

BIG SIS *(to* **LITTLE MISS***)* In the UK, the third Sunday in June celebrates the role of which parent?

L.M Mother.

BIG SIS Incorrect, the correct answer is father. (*To* **LIL' SIS**) In music, which song off Michael Jackson's album Bad is Mum's favourite?

LIL' SIS The way you make me feel.

BIG SIS Correct.

LI'L SIS Bank.

---

1 A license to produce LITTLE MISS BURDEN does not include a performance license for any third-party or copyrighted music. Licensees should create an original composition or use music in the public domain. For further information, please see Music Use Note on page iii.

BIG SIS *(to* **LITTLE MISS***)* In history, on 28th of March 1951 which influential man was born in Okiti Pupa, Ondo State, Nigeria?

L.M I don't know. Pass.

BIG SIS Incorrect, the correct answer is your dad.

L.M Excuse me?

BIG SIS I mean the correct answer is our father.

L.M Oh. I didn't know that. *(To* **LIL' SIS***)* Did you?

LIL' SIS *shrugs her shoulder.*

BIG SIS *(to* **LIL' SIS***)* Name the process of movement of material, along a coast by waves, which approach at an angle to the coast edge, but are received directly away from it.

L.M What? That's your question.

LIL' SIS *and* **LITTLE MISS** *share a confused look.*

LIL' SIS Longshore drift.

BIG SIS Correct.

LIL' SIS Bank.

BIG SIS *(to* **LITTLE MISS***)* In history, which –

Pips signal the end of the round.

– I've started so I shall finish, which infamous figure had one mother, two fathers, and twelve best friends.

L.M Jesus Christ – I don't know – is that even possible?

BIG SIS Correct. That round you banked a miserable seventy-five pounds. Which disciple is financially betraying the group, it's time to vote off the—

Video game warp sound effect.[2]

---

2 A license to produce LITTLE MISS BURDEN does not include a performance license for any third-party or copyrighted sound effects. Licensees should create their own.

WORLD 7 – SEE YOU AT THE CHRIST-ROADS

A song in the style of Uche Agu ***"MY GOD IS GOOD"*** [1]*plays as the volume gradually increases.*

The rhythmic drums in the song dissolve the previous scene and enter the bodies of Anne and Contestant, as they dance and are taken over by the music they morph into **PASTOR** *and* **INTERPRETER.**

LITTLE MISS *is transported back to reality and is not impressed.*

BIG SIS *and* **LIL' SIS** *put white gowns and caps (the type worn at C&S churches) on each other like surgeons.* **BIG SIS** *wears a red sash.* **LIL' SIS** *wears a green sash. They tie a rainbow coloured rope around each other's waist.*

PASTOR *and* **INTERPRETER** *bring handkerchiefs out of their pockets and wave them around as they dance, hearts full for praise and worship.*

INTERPRETER *slaps her handkerchief into* **LITTLE MISS'***s face and she is instantly sucked back into the real world.*

---

1 A license to produce LITTLE MISS BURDEN does not include a performance license for "My God is Good" The publisher and author suggest that the licensee contact PRS to ascertain the music publisher and contact such music publisher to license or acquire permission for performance of the song. If a license or permission is unattainable for "MY God is Good", the licensee may not use the song in LITTLE MISS BURDEN but should create an original composition in a similar style or use a similar song in the public domain. For further information, please see Music Use Note on page iii.

LITTLE MISS'*s bold demeanour shrinks at the weight of Christ, God and not forgetting the Holy Spirit.*

BIG SIS Cherubim and Seraphim–

LIL SIS AKA white gown church–

L.M Age eleven–

PASTOR Thank you Jesus.

INTERPRETER *Kabiyesi o seun.*

PASTOR I want you to turn to your neighbour and say you are the opening act but Almighty God –

INTERPRETER – *mimo* –

PASTOR –is the headliner.

ALL Turn to your neighbour and say you are the opening act but Almighty God is the headliner.

INTERPRETER *looks around searching.* **LITTLE MISS** *tries to sink into her seat.*

PASTOR I have a message for somebody in this room. I received an important message for somebody in this room from the Most High. I feel the spirit coming express delivery.

INTERPRETER Where Pastor?

PASTOR From the East to West. From the North to the South. And all around.

INTERPRETER Can somebody shout Amen?

ALL Amen!

PASTOR Hmm-mmm... Please bring her to the front?

LITTLE MISS *is reluctantly ushered to the front of the altar.*

Do you believe in our Lord and Saviour Jesus Christ?

L.M Yes.

PASTOR Do you believe you will run again?

L.M ...I mean I haven't for years.

PASTOR You will run faster than Denise Lewis. You will strut taller than Naomi Campbell for all to bear witness to the power of the Almighty. Can somebody shout Hallelujah?!

ALL Hallelujah!

PASTOR Any time you are doubting – I want you to say to yourself: I am blessed and I will be healed. Let me hear you say it.

L.M *(mumbles)* I am blessed and I will be healed.

PASTOR Say it like you mean it. Say it like you believe it. I want you to speak it into existence!

L.M I am blessed and I will be healed.

PASTOR And again.

PASTOR *takes* **LITTLE MISS** *by the hand.*

PASTOR/L.M I am blessed and I will be healed!

PASTOR You've heard our daughter – let us seal this blessing in prayer.

PASTOR *rests his hand on* **LITTLE MISS***'s head.*

The Almighty revealed to me that your health is taking a new shape today. Say it to your neighbour.

PASTOR *and* **INTERPRETER** *encourage the audience to talk to their neighbour.*

ALL Your health is taking a new shape today.

The **INTERPRETER** *wipes the brow of the* **PASTOR**, *but goes a little overboard with the handkerchief.* **PASTOR** *snatches the handkerchief from the* **INTERPRETER**.

PASTOR Thank you Jesus. *(Jogs around* **LITTLE MISS***)* You will run into your testimony.

The **INTERPRETER** *jogs a lap around the* **PASTOR.**

I said you will run into your testimony.

INTERPRETER Hallelujah!

The **INTERPRETER** *does a single burpee.*

PASTOR You will be restored whole.

INTERPRETER Amin Jesu.

PASTOR *waits for* **INTERPRETER** *to perform an action but the* **INTERPRETER** *holds their side, as she is out of breath. She waves the* **PASTOR** *to continue their sermon.*

PASTOR *goes into the audience.*

PASTOR Can you all raise your hands for me?

PASTOR *encourages the audience to raise an arm.*

Now direct your hands to our daughter here.

PASTOR *encourages the audience to point their hands towards* **LITTLE MISS** *who looks away embarrassed.*

Repeat after me. This sickness –

AUDIENCE This sickness –

PASTOR – does not belong to you –

AUDIENCE – does not belong to you–

PASTOR – return it to Mr Satan –

AUDIENCE – return it to Mr Satan –

PASTOR – now go ahead and pray that prayer. I bind and cast this sickness out of you. Ring-ring. Delivery for Mr Satan! Take it back! Accept it! It is yours! It is yours! It is yours!

WORLD 8 – LA CASERA FALLS

BIG SIS Nigeria

LIL' SIS Ketu, Lagos

L.M Age eleven and three quarters

LIL' SIS Age seven

BIG SIS Age sixteen

BIG SIS Eight suitcases and three hand luggages

L.M Eleven hour journey from Hackney to Ketu

LIL' SIS My first time on a plane

L.M My first time using my passport

BIG SIS My first time back home in over a decade

L.M Mum tells us to dress for the plane

LIL' SIS What does that mean?

BIG SIS It'll be cold on the plane but hot when we land

LIL' SIS How's that even possible? Is Nigeria even a real place?

L.M It has to be. We've all been taking these tablets because of a disease called

LIL' SIS Malteasers

L.M It's called Naira

BIG SIS It's called malaria, you coconut heads. Naira is Nigeria's currency

LIL' SIS They're disgusting – we have to take like six tablets a day for eight weeks

L.M And we have to be on the lookout for mosquitos because they carry the disease

LIL' SIS I don't know what a mosquito looks like

L.M We can ask the police when we get there

BIG SIS *kisses her teeth.*

BIG SIS Mum tells us Nigeria is one hour ahead so we'll be arriving there in the evening

LIL' SIS Does that mean they move an hour faster?

L.M How do you catch up because I can't run anymore?

BIG SIS See what I have to put up with. This is why I didn't want to be sat next to either of them on the plane.

LIL' SIS Oh my God. The plane is driving!

L.M I didn't know you can drive a plane like a car!

LIL' SIS *(shouts)* I think we're going to crash!

BIG SIS We're just taking off

LIL' SIS *(shouts)* My ears hurt!

L.M I'm so hungry

BIG SIS They're going to bring food soon

LIL' SIS *(shouts)* What?!

L.M How? There's no kitchen.

LIL' SIS Food is here

BIG SIS Chicken in custard?

L.M Or vegetarian Kiev?

LIL' SIS Mum if there's a kitchen here, can you make us something to eat?

LIL' SIS We fall asleep –

L.M – from hunger –

They all scream.

LIL' SIS The person in front leans their chair back spilling my orange juice into my lap.

ALL *Oloshi!*

L.M It's official. We hate flying.

LIL' SIS The plane is rumbling – we're going to crash!

BIG SIS We're landing

L.M Where's that heat coming from, Mum?

MUM That is Lagos!

A song in the style of Lagbaja ***"SKENTELE SKONTOLO"***[1] *plays.*

The **SISTERS** *put on geles and dance like Nigerian aunties at a wedding, spraying each other with Monopoly notes.*

The song can play in the background of this scene.

Soundscape of bustling car engines and horns, the rustle of motorbike exhausts and the chatter of street sellers and their customers. Above all the sounds is the constant hum of a generator.

BIG SIS As the airport waves us goodbye

---

1 A license to produce LITTLE MISS BURDEN does not include a performance license for "Skentele Skontolo" The publisher and author suggest that the licensee contact PRS to ascertain the music publisher and contact such music publisher to license or acquire permission for performance of the song. If a license or permission is unattainable for "Skentele Skontolo", the licensee may not use the song in LITTLE MISS BURDEN but should create an original composition in a similar style or use a similar song in the public domain. For further information, please see Music Use Note on page iii.

L.M We are bombarded by men offering to help us with our luggage

LIL' SIS An old lady approaches mum

L.M Who is that?

BIG SIS I don't know.

MUM This is my mum. Come and greet your grandma.

LIL' SIS Wait. You have a mum?

BIG SIS Of course she does!

LIL' SIS But Mum is old. How old is Grandma?

BIG SIS You can't ask her that.

L.M Grandma hugs everyone but when she comes to me, she holds my face and draws my forehead to her lips. She smells of stew and perfume.

GRANDMA *Oko mi.* How are you?

L.M I'm fine Grandma.

GRANDMA *Se o gbo Yoruba?*

L.M Grandma asks me. Yeah, a little bit.

MUM They understand. They just can't speak it.

L.M She takes my luggage and clasps my hand as we make our way to the taxi rank.

BIG SIS As colourful as Nigeria is during the day, its real personality comes out at night.

LIL' SIS Which can be a bit scary to the unexperienced traveller.

BIG SIS Because there aren't really any street lights.

LIL' SIS At least where Grandma lives.

L.M But who needs lights when you can have stars.

All the **SISTERS** *have a dance off, showcasing their differently styled geles.*

The song gradually begins to fade away.

Sounds of the busy streets of Lagos as **MUM** *and* **LITTLE MISS** *sit in a taxi.*

Are we Lagosians Mum?

MUM Of course.

L.M Even though we weren't born here?

MUM Yes we are Lagosians and Londoners.

L.M Mum?

L.M Why couldn't Big Sis and Lil' Sis come with us?

MUM They are helping Grandma make dinner.

L.M I could help Grandma.

MUM I know but this is important.

L.M Is it always this hot?

MUM Hot *ke*? This is our raining season.

L.M Does everyone speak English here?

MUM Of course. And some speak Pidgin.

L.M They can talk to birds?

MUM No. Don't go around asking that.

L.M Then how do they know English?

MUM It's a long story, one I'm sure you'll learn about in school.

ALL We didn't.

L.M Where we were going was far. I had fallen asleep and woken up and we still weren't there yet.

A smiling **HERBALIST** *appears, barefoot and wearing an agbada. He blesses all who enter his space with incense.*

Who's that?

MUM Shh...walk behind me.

He leads **LITTLE MISS** *and* **MUM** *into the centre of the room.* **MUM** *kneels and bows her head.*

HERBALIST *Oluwa lon fun ogbon, ki se eniyan*

MUM *Kabiyesi Olodumare.*

L.M What is he saying?

HERBALIST God gives us wisdom not man.

L.M You speak English?

HERBALIST *smiles and nods.*

Can you talk to pigeons?

MUM Hey, what did I say?

HERBALIST *grinds plants in a pestle and mortar.* **HERBALIST** *empties the contents into a cup.*

HERBALIST *raises the cup to the sky.*

HERBALIST *Ewe nje ogun ti o je ewe ni o pe.*

MUM Herbs that do not work means the recipe is not complete.

HERBALIST *hands the cup to* **LITTLE MISS** *and gives her a nod that says 'drink'.*

LITTLE MISS *takes the cup.*

L.M I don't want to.

MUM It's good for you.

L.M Doesn't smell good.

MUM *Oko mi.* Please drink it, its medicine.

LITTLE MISS *looks to* **MUM** *who nods. She drinks the cup's contents.*

HERBALIST *Agbo ti o n mu yi a tu e lara*

MUM The herbs you are drinking will bring you relief.

LITTLE MISS *finishes drinking the cup. She winces at the bitter taste.*

Video game warp sound effect[1]

BIG SIS *breaks character as* **HERBALIST.**

BIG SIS What did it taste like?

L.M You know that concoction Mum gives us when we have a stomach ache.

LIL' SIS *breaks character as* **MUM.**

ALL Jedi-jedi.

BIG SIS Jedi-jedi tasted like soil mixed with –

LIL' SIS – blended tree.

ALL Ughhh.

L.M Basically it tasted like something you shouldn't drink... bitter on the tongue but got worse with each swallow.

Video game warp sound effect[2]

BIG SIS *and* **LIL' SIS** *resume roles.*

MUM *rubs creams into* **LITTLE MISS***'s body. She does so calmly and lovingly. She stretches her fingers and arms.*

This smells nice.

MUM It's blessed oil.

HERBALIST *Omo ki i ku l'owo onikola*

MUM A child does not die while being cared for.

---

1 A license to produce LITTLE MISS BURDEN does not include a performance license for any third-party or copyrighted sound effects. Licensees should create their own.

2 A license to produce LITTLE MISS BURDEN does not include a performance license for any third-party or copyrighted sound effects. Licensees should create their own.

L.M Why does he have a blade?

MUM Calm down.

L.M Mum.

MUM It's just so that the medicine can get inside your body.

L.M I drank the tea. I drank it all. I'll drink it again.

MUM Hey, you remember the injections, the doctor gives you. It's like that. Doesn't hurt, only stings.

L.M Mum please.

MUM Don't you want to get better? We came all this way. We took a plane, a car and trekked to get here. This is all for you.

L.M I thought it was a holiday.

MUM It is. After we do this, okay? Be the strong girl, I know that you are.

LITTLE MISS *nods.*

HERBALIST *takes* **LITTLE MISS***'s arm and she flinches.* **HERBALIST** *uses a blade and make several tiny incisions around* **LITTLE MISS***'s elbow and ankles.* **HERBALIST** *then rubs black ash into the incisions.*

HERBALIST *Àjèjé owo kan ko gbe igbá. de ori*

L.M I'll be better, right?

MUM Much better, by God's grace.

HERBALIST Omo ki iku lo'owo onikola

MUM *and* **HERBALIST***'s chants rain on* **LITTLE MISS** *like blessings from God herself.*

Ara a tu e

MUM You will be healed.

HERBALIST *War in bi Olorun se da e*

MUM You will walk, as God has made you.

HERBALIST *Ara a tu e…*

Ara a tu e…

Ara a tu e…

Ara a tu e…

HERBALIST *and* **MUM**'*s voices dissolve into the night.*

LITTLE MISS *is sat beside* **MUM** *in the back of a taxi. The hum of the engine sits between them.*

L.M Who was that man Mummy?

MUM A herbalist.

L.M Oh like Bulbasaur.

MUM – who?

L.M A Pokémon.

MUM It's not like your cartoon. This is serious.

L.M I know. It's like when Sailor Moon finds out she has a child called Rini who she forgets because an evil witch attacks and curses her kingdom in the future, so her daughter travels back in time to warn her, so Sailor Moon and the Sailor Scouts can try to stop the future witch in the past. But first Rini has to convince Sailor Moon in the past that she is her future daughter. It's that serious.

MUM …Yes.

L.M What's wrong with me?

MUM Nothing… You just have a medical condition.

L.M I have a medical condition.

MUM And it will leave in Jesus' name.

L.M It doesn't feel like it wants to leave.

MUM It will, but you have to believe.

L.M Then it will go? Just like that?

MUM Yes. Because I serve a living God who is in the miracle business. So we must never give up.

LGMD And I've just opened for business.

L.M I didn't want Mum to think I was giving up, so I didn't tell her when the pain went from bad to really really bad.

WORLD 9 – NO PRICE TOO HIGH MOUNTAIN

The **SISTERS** *behave like QVC presenters but on acid.*

BIG SIS Tonic water is good for your muscles

ALL Good for your muscles

ALL Good for your muscles

L.M Garlic and ginger is good for your muscles

ALL Good for your muscles

ALL Good for your muscles

LIL' SIS Blessed oil is good for your muscles

ALL Good for your muscles

ALL Good for your muscles

BIG SIS Haliborange is good for your muscles

ALL Good for your muscles

ALL Good for your muscles

L.M Swimming is good for your muscles

ALL Good for your muscles

ALL Good for your muscles

LIL' SIS Smiling is good for your muscles

ALL Good for your muscles

ALL Good for your muscles

BIG SIS Wrapping up in winter is good for your muscles

ALL Good for your muscles

ALL Good for your muscles

L.M Bottling up emotions is good for your muscles

ALL Good for your muscles

ALL Good for your muscles

LIL' SIS Staying away from dogs is good for your muscles

ALL Good for your muscles

ALL Good for your muscles

BIG SIS Cinnamon is good for your muscles

L.M Disney films are good for your muscles

LIL' SIS Driving over potholes is good for your muscles

BIG SIS PlayStation is good for your muscles

L.M Castles are good for your muscles

LIL' SIS Candy floss is good for your muscles

L.M Panic attacks are good for your muscles

BIG SIS This mysterious Chinese herb is good for your muscles

L.M What's in it?

LIL' SIS We don't know, but what we do know is...it's

ALL Good for your muscles
Good for your muscles
Good for your muscles

BIG SIS And all of these wonderful items could be yours for the low low price of your dignity –

LIL' SIS – respect –

BIG SIS – confidence –

LIL' SIS – price doesn't include VAG –

BIG SIS – value-added guilt, once purchased items are non-refundable.

WORLD 10 – STAIRCASE TO HEAVEN

Instrumental version of R&B upbeat music plays.

School bell rings.

BIG SIS Homerton

LIL' SIS Secondary school

L.M Age twelve and a half

BIG SIS This is where I love you and leave you.

L.M Where you going?

BIG SIS University.

LIL' SIS Can I come?

BIG SIS Uh – no! Finally I don't have to share a room and can come and go as I please.

MUM I want you to study hard and graduate.

BIG SIS I will. I will. See you later losers.

L.M I'm going to miss her but don't tell her I said that.

LIL' SIS Of all the schools in Hackney, course, Mum would choose the Catholic one.

L.M Mum didn't want her daughters to grow up wayward.

MUM God is the best testimonial for any school.

L.M Did he say that, to you? Mum smiles and hands me a box. What is it?

MUM Open it.

L.M It's a – it's a mobile phone! Oh my God! A Sagem myX-2. It looks expensive -

LIL' SIS – it's from Woolworths.

L.M It has a colour screen, four games, a calculator and ten pound credit. Jesus.

LIL' SIS I want a phone!

L.M Who you calling, Rosie and Jim? I already feel like an adult. I set my ringtone to, well, the only tune on there.

They sing a song in the style of Kylie Minogue – ***"CAN'T GET YOU OUT OF MY HEAD".***[1]

The **SISTERS** *share a confused look.*

LIL' SIS And an incredibly excited Little Miss was now running late.

L.M The playground was eerily empty and quiet like in those western films. I could already feel the judgement in the atmosphere, seeping into my pores, whispering –

ALL – sinner, sinner, sinner -

L.M – into my soul.

MUM Let's see if we can find a teacher... Excuse me, Miss.

TEACHER Parents are not allowed to escort students beyond the fence unless you have an appointment.

---

1 A license to produce LITTLE MISS BURDEN does not include a performance license for "Can't Get You Out Of My Head" The publisher and author suggest that the licensee contact PRS to ascertain the music publisher and contact such music publisher to license or acquire permission for performance of the song. If a license or permission is unattainable for "Can't Get You Out Of My Head", the licensee may not use the song in LITTLE MISS BURDEN but should create an original composition in a similar style or use a similar song in the public domain. For further information, please see Music Use Note on page iii.

MUM I just wanted to let you know that she may need assistance –

TEACHER – are those heels? We have a no heels, no hoops and no outlandish hair policy at this school.

MUM They are not heels, they help her walk.

TEACHER Why? What's wrong with her?

MUM Nothing. She just needs a little more time getting around –

TEACHER – should have come on time then. This school will straighten her out. They've already started assembly in the gymnasium. Follow me.

MUM Have a good day. I'll see you at three o'clock.

L.M Mum...please...wait... I...

TEACHER Up the stairs and on your right.

L.M Is there a lift?

TEACHER Lift? Don't be so lazy. Up you go.

L.M I push the heavy glass door and I'm instantly met with a familiar foe. My nemesis... the staircase. I've never seen this many stairs in my life. This school has more stairs than Hogwarts. I begin to climb the mountain of stairs. Each step sapping energy from my muscles, pain coursing through my body like a train, making no stops. When I finally reach the summit, hot and out of breath, I wait a moment to catch my breath, just as I am about to enter the gymnasium, the teacher stand holding the door open.

TEACHER Take off your shoes.

L.M No.

TEACHER What did you say?

L.M Why?

TEACHER Because I said so.

L.M I can't.

TEACHER Take them off.

L.M I couldn't tell her what lay under my adapted shoes.

TEACHER All pupils must take off their shoes in the gymnasium. Do you want to be sent to the Head Teacher's office on your first day?

L.M I picked up my shoes and held them. I could feel the cold floor through my tights. As I tried to enter quietly on my toes, I realised there was no way of sneaking into the assembly and so like an ungraceful ballerina I took to the stage. The sea of whispers raged across the room, drowning out the teacher addressing everyone.

PUPILS Why is she walking like that?

L.M *(whispers)* And I say hey! What a wonderful kind of day.

PUPILS What's wrong with her feet?

Stifled sniggers.

L.M *(whispers)* You can learn to work and play.

PUPILS Oh my god.

L.M *(whispers)* And get along with each other.

PUPILS Can you see what she's doing?

Cheeky chuckles.

What's wrong with her?

She's walking like that on purpose.

Loud laughter.

TEACHER Sit down right this instant.

L.M Could I sit on the bench? I can't sit on the floor.

TEACHER Fine –

L.M – I sit down, clenching my jaw so tight to stop the sea of tears bursting out from my eyes. Whilst my teeth were moments from shattering, I slowly tried to use my Umbro backpack to cover the attention my feet were getting. Because unlike a ballerina, people weren't staring in amazement but rather bewilderment.

In school I'm referred to as:

LIL' SIS Captain Moron

L.M Peg leg

BIG SIS Hunchback

L.M Slut

BIG SIS Loser

L.M *(Little Britain impersonation)* I want that one

LIL' SIS Fucking freak

L.M Sinner

BIG SIS I'd kill myself if I walked like her

LIL' SIS I heard it's contagious

L.M Mong

BIG SIS Trinity from Matrix

L.M That's actually a compliment

LIL' SIS Fat bastard

L.M That isn't

BIG SIS Witch

L.M Black bitch

LIL' SIS Smelly bitch

BIG SIS Bitch bitch

LIL' SIS Blackie

L.M Ugly

LIL' SIS Just plain evil

BIG SIS She's cursed

LIL' SIS She's faking

BIG SIS Attention seeker

L.M People would ask me if I knew who my real mum and dad were because no one else in my family were like me, so I must be

BIG SIS Retard

LIL' SIS N-word

L.M Not normal

BIG SIS That's not the N-word

L.M I was called the other one too

LIL' SIS And the C-word

L.M Cripple

BIG SIS That's also not the C-word

L.M What's the word for when you're all of the above?

BIG SIS Dumb

LIL' SIS Stupid

BIG SIS Pathetic

LIL' SIS Idiot

TEACHER Well I don't think we've ever had a *[bleep]* student enrolled before?

L.M What's the name when everyone hates all these traits individually but despises them even more, if they come rolled into one?

LIL' SIS I don't like this part.

BIG SIS We have to.

LIL' SIS Can't we make it happier, funnier, less –

BIG SIS We promised. Stick to the facts.

LIL' SIS ...

BIG SIS Little Miss found a way to cope with the constant bullying and isolation. She'd eat all her feelings including hope. She began stealing coins from Mum's purse.

LIL' SIS She'd skip school dinners and buy snacks on the way home.

BIG SIS She'd go on a shopping spree in the local offie. She'd buy frosties sweets –

LIL' SIS – cola flavour –

BIG SIS – Nik Naks –

LIL' SIS – nice and spicy –

BIG SIS – muffins –

LIL' SIS – double chocolate chip –

BIG SIS – sherbet, astro-belts, Panda Pops –

LIL' SIS – or apple Tango if they ran out.

BIG SIS She was always the first home and so had a small window to savour her treats.

LIL' SIS She'd eat it all in one sitting.

BIG SIS Her stomach hurting from the pressure.

LIL' SIS She'd eat Mum's dinner full and in pain. Then one day a teacher found Little Miss crying alone in a classroom.

TEACHER Are you ok?

L.M Yes Miss... Sorry I'll leave.

TEACHER Do you want to tell me what's upsetting you?

LITTLE MISS *shakes her head.*

Ok. How about you write it?

LITTLE MISS *shakes her head.*

You don't have to write what's happening, but tell me how it makes you feel. You can write it as a letter, a story or a poem? Only I will read it, no one else. I promise. Can you do that for me?

LITTLE MISS *shrugs her shoulders.*

Doesn't have to be long at all. Just a few sentences. Have you ever heard of Helen Keller?

LITTLE MISS *shakes her head.*

She was a deaf-blind author.

L.M She was deaf and blind?

TEACHER Yes.

L.M How did she write a book–

TEACHER – twelve.

L.M She wrote twelve books?

TEACHER With help from her teacher called Anne Sullivan who was also partially sighted. They developed a language together so that they could understand each other.

L.M But I'm not blind or deaf.

TEACHER I know that but as a *(bleep)* student, I want to find a way I can understand you better.

L.M When I got home. I sat at the dining table to do my secret homework. I looked up the word *(bleep)* in the dictionary. I didn't quite understand its meaning.

What is an injury without an event?

Does that mean your injury doesn't mean what it's meant

Physically plus mentally equals something wrong with me

But if you divide me in half, you'll find I live alone in this body

Mum what does *(bleep)* mean?

MUM Where did you hear that word?

L.M Miss called me it at school. She said I was a *(bleep)* student. What does she mean?

MUM It is a word...to describe...it is a collective term to –

L.M – collective?

MUM A word used to describe a group...of people who –

L.M – so me, Big Sis and Lil' Sis. We're *(bleep)*?

MUM No. I think...your teacher was referring to your condition.

L.M My condition is *(bleep)*?

MUM Yes...it is *(bleep)*-ing.

L.M So I'm not *(bleep)*. My condition is?

MUM You are not a *(bleep)* girl. You have a medical condition.

L.M Ok...but –

MUM – even teachers can get things wrong sometimes.

L.M I don't understand. Am I *(bleep)* or not?

WORLD 11 – NO RETURNS POLICY

L.M The real scare of my life came roaring into my underwear shortly after my thirteenth birthday.

BIG SIS TMI, sis.

LIL' SIS Hey we are three girls remember, together we've probably shed more blood than Christ. Speak your truth, sis!

L.M Over a year into secondary school and I was a teenager, basically a step closer to adulthood and a step closer to leaving this Hellmouth. For this important birthday I didn't receive my first kiss via a brutal game of spin the bottle and I didn't get the remote controlled helicopter I specifically asked for from Argos. No instead I got the "the talk" from Mum.

MUM You are a woman now. It means you are growing up. So I'm going to talk to you like a grown up.

LITTLE MISS *nods.*

You know what having your period means...mhmmm, so don't be doing any dilly dally with any boy or man for that matter because you will end up what?

MUM *holds her ear.*

L.M ...Pregnant.

MUM Mhmmmm, and I cannot allow that. You will not make me a grandmother at my age when my own mother is still alive... Ehnn, so listen well-well. Don't do hmmm with any hmmmm because you will fall hmmm. Ok.

LITTLE MISS *nods.*

I can't hear you.

L.M Yes Mum...

MUM Now go and rest, I will bring you a hot water bottle.

L.M My thirteenth birthday also brought the biggest gift of all... Lamb Griddle Muscule-car Disk-trophy.

LGMD Who's that?

BIG SIS Limbo Girl Musical Discography.

LGMD Huh. Nope, that's even worse.

LIL' SIS Lime Garlic Mussel Delicacy.

LGMD It's Limb Girdle Muscular Dystrophy. Limb Girdle Muscular Dystrophy. Now say it with me!

A deeply unsettling voice joins in.

ALL Limb Girdle Muscular Dystrophy!

LGMD Thank you for the lukewarm welcome. That's my government name – but my posse – call me LGMD.

A song is played in the style of Destiny's Child's – ***"BOOTYLICIOUS"***[1]*.*

BIG SIS, LIL' SIS *and* **LITTLE MISS** *dance to the song but are put off by the lyrics.*

LGMD *sings a song in the style of Destiny's Child's –* ***"BOOTYLICIOUS"****, inserting the characters' names .*

L.M So finally came a formal diagnosis to Limb Girdle Muscular Dystrophy. A gift I couldn't return. A rumour that I heard of for some time but I now had proof was true.

---

1 A license to produce LITTLE MISS BURDEN does not include a performance license for "Bootylicious" The publisher and author suggest that the licensee contact PRS to ascertain the music publisher and contact such music publisher to license or acquire permission for performance of the song. If a license or permission is unattainable for "Bootylicious", the licensee may not use the song in LITTLE MISS BURDEN but should create an original composition in a similar style or use a similar song in the public domain. For further information, please see Music Use Note on page iii.

BIG SIS *puts on an announcer voice in Bruce Forsythe's The Price is Right. Whilst* **LIL' SIS** *is the silent glamourous model demonstrating each prize.*

BIG SIS Little Miss come on down. Let's take a look at what excellent prizes you've won.

Walking with a waddle because of weakness of the hip and leg muscles.

Walking like a ditzy penguin.

LIL' SIS *imaginatively demonstrates.*

BIG SIS Trouble standing from chairs, a toilet seat or climbing stairs.

L.M It's like your bum gets glued to anything it touches.

LIL' SIS *imaginatively demonstrates.*

BIG SIS Weakness in the shoulder muscles meaning difficulty raising your arms over your head or carrying objects.

L.M You develop butter fingers and spaghetti arms.

LGMD Cooked spaghetti.

LIL' SIS *imaginatively demonstrates.*

BIG SIS It becomes increasingly hard to do activities like combing your hair, doing your make up, brushing your teeth, even feeding yourself.

L.M My hands and head repel each other like magnets.

LIL' SIS *demonstrates.*

BIG SIS The heart and lungs may decline over time, though this isn't the case for everyone.

BIG SIS and **LIL' SIS** Sadly the condition doesn't affect sensation, digestion, bowels, bladder, sexual function or intellect.

BIG SIS Better luck next time.

A snippet of game show music plays.

WORLD 12 - PEN ISLAND

School bell rings.

BIG SIS Secondary school

LIL' SIS Age fourteen

L.M The rumours at school kept people away from me

BIG SIS She's such a liar.

LIL' SIS I've seen her run for a bus, and sit on the top deck.

BIG SIS She's being punished for her ancestors, sins.

LIL' SIS She was supposed to die at birth but didn't.

L.M If I'm so bad, then why do I try so hard to be good?

CJ Do you want me to carry your PE bag?

L.M I'll be fine.

CJ Are you sure?

L.M Yeah, thanks though.

CJ I'm stronger than I look.

L.M Ohh-k...

CJ See look. Feel my arm. Go on feel it.

LITTLE MISS *feels* **CJ**'s *bicep.*

L.M Solid.

CJ Let me take your bag.

L.M Thanks. I'm –

CJ I know who you are. Everyone knows who you are.

L.M Yeah course. What's your name again?

CJ CJ.

L.M Sailor Jupiter.

CJ Who?

L.M Nothing. Do you like Gwen Stefani?

CJ Yeah. Why?

L.M CJ had porcelain skin, the longest hair I'd ever seen on a human before. It was even longer than Mum's. She was statuesque and had a smile that always made me smile even when I didn't want to.

LIL' SIS And so two and a bit years into secondary school, Little Miss made her first friend.

L.M Don't say it like that. It makes me sound like a loser. I assure you I wasn't. CJ was more than a friend. She was my Gwen Stefani.

CJ And she was my Eve.

L.M Before we could get settled in our personas we were joined by our third member –

LIL' SIS – Selin.

L.M Selin was a proud Turkish delight of a person. Took pride in her appearance, make-up, piercings and Turkish culture. What she lacked in height she made up for in buckets attitude.

SELIN *mimic raps in the style of SLK's –* ***"HYPE HYPE".***[1]

---

1 A license to produce LITTLE MISS BURDEN does not include a performance license for "Hype Hype" The publisher and author suggest that the licensee contact PRS to ascertain the music publisher and contact such music publisher to license or acquire permission for performance of the song. If a license or permission is unattainable for "Hype Hype", the licensee may not use the song in LITTLE MISS BURDEN but should create an original composition in a similar style or use a similar song in the public domain. For further information, please see Music Use Note on page iii.

SELIN Too many peng tings in that video. Made me wet just watching them.

They burst into fits of laughter.

L.M I'm laughing like I know what wet means – I don't.

CJ I would sit on SLK's face all day, every day, like even on my period.

L.M But why...would you do that?

CJ *and* **SELIN** *look at each other and burst into laughter.*

A song in the style of Salt-N-Pepa's – ***"LET'S TALK ABOUT SEX"*** *plays.*[1]

Little did I realise how much I didn't know about sex. The stuff they shared with me blew my mind. Like...

CJ You don't always have to wear a condom.

SELIN Or be married.

L.M Yeah I know that. I was four when my parents got married.

CJ Bastard. *(High fives* **LITTLE MISS***)* Welcome to the club.

SELIN Mary wasn't exactly a virgin.

CJ We meet fortnightly for Bastard Brunches.

SELIN Have you heard of the Kama Sutra?

L.M Err...

CJ Dildo

---

1 A license to produce LITTLE MISS BURDEN does not include a performance license for "Let's Talk About Sex" The publisher and author suggest that the licensee contact PRS to ascertain the music publisher and contact such music publisher to license or acquire permission for performance of the song. If a license or permission is unattainable for "Let's Talk About Sex", the licensee may not use the song in LITTLE MISS BURDEN but should create an original composition in a similar style or use a similar song in the public domain. For further information, please see Music Use Note on page iii.

SELIN Scissoring if you're into girls

L.M Is that when you run with scissors...but like in a sexy way?

CJ Do you know what cum is?

SELIN Squirting

L.M Like with water guns? Yeah I got a couple at home.

CJ Giving head

SELIN Going down on a girl

CJ Anal

SELIN Fingering

L.M Yeah... That's – that's when, you use chocolate fingers to-to you know, stir it in-inside.

SELIN You're not a good liar.

CJ Like, the worst.

SELIN Top ten things you should know about sex. Take notes.

CJ No one does missionary

SELIN You can't get pregnant on your period

CJ We can make yeast

SELIN Sometimes your period smells like red bull

CJ So you should eat more pineapples, if you're gonna have period sex

SELIN And watermelon

CJ You can fit two in at a time or even a whole fist

SELIN Choking's totally normal – guys like that

CJ Apparently if you swallow, you won't feel hungry for like hours

SELIN Every time you sneeze you orgasm

L.M I couldn't understand why they liked me but they did and I liked them too.

WORLD 13 – TRICK OR TREAT(MENT)

BIG SIS *and* **LIL' SIS** *set up hospital set.*

BIG SIS Paddington

LIL' SIS Queen Mary's Hospital

L.M Age fifteen and thirty nine days

SURGEON We are going to perform an operation called a tendon release on both her ankles. This will help her walk with a bit more ease. Improve her posture and get her heels to touch the ground.

MUM She will walk properly?

SURGEON Yes.

MUM *Oluwa şeun.* What will the tendon release entail?

(Thank God)

SURGEON It involves us severing her tendon then reattaching it very loosely to allow for a greater range of movement in her ankle. It's a routine procedure and I have performed them the world over.

MUM And what about recovery?

SURGEON Typically six to eight weeks. She will need physiotherapy and leg splints to help her walk again. But then she should be walking normally from then on.

MUM You hear that? You will walk properly. Aren't you happy?

L.M Yeah... Mum had made it her mission to get me better for the past eight years. She didn't sit twiddling her thumbs waiting for medicine to catch up. She was Lara Croft – no – she was *Omolara Croft* on a mission and she'd found the cure.

For me.

I couldn't remember a time when I hadn't walked with my heel above the ground. My heels had spent more than half my life looking down from above.

I wasn't happy...

I was ecstatic. Over the moon and hurtling through the galaxy on joy. Except months off school – I hoped CJ and Selin wouldn't forget me.

My mind was rocketing at all the things I would be able to do.

A video game level up sound effect after each achievement.[1]

BIG SIS Run faster than a lightning bolt with scissors

L.M Leap higher than a leap year over Lil' Sis

LIL' SIS Run up the steps of Hackney Town Hall like Rocky

BIG SIS Hula hoop and Double Dutch in the playground

L.M Climb the apparatus in the gymnasium

LIL' SIS Play Dance Dance Revolution

BIG SIS Play Rounders

L.M Ice Skating at Lea Valley

LIL' SIS Do the Cha-Cha slide but like properly

BIG SIS Wear normal shoes – sayonara orthopaedic shoes!

L.M I hated you so much! I'm going to be like my sisters. It's not long before word gets around school.

CJ So if you can walk properly, then you'll be fine. You know all the boys are going to fancy you, you bitch.

L.M Yeah, I will.

---

1 A license to produce LITTLE MISS BURDEN does not include a performance license for any third-party or copyrighted sound effects. Licensees should create their own.

SELIN So you'll be able to run like us?

CJ You know what that means. You're going to have to do PE with us, in those ugly shorts?

L.M Oh yeah. I will be cat walking in them shorts.

SELIN We're going to out every weekend once you're better.

CJ I'm going to take you to a rave.

SELIN I'm going to take you to Thorpe Park.

CJ I'm going to take you to dine and dash at an fancy restaurant like Pizza Express.

SELIN I'm going to take you to an orgy.

They all burst into laughter.

L.M I cannot wait to do all of that.

CJ You're a miracle, you know that right? Like I didn't think they were real until I met you.

A song in the style of Boney M's – ***"MARY'S BOY CHILD"*** *plays.*[1]

L.M Christmas felt different this year. First time I didn't really want anything. I'm getting something you can't exactly gift wrap. In the New Year – I'm going to actually be new.

The **SISTERS** *pull Christmas Crackers.*

They do a dance to the song.

---

1 A license to produce LITTLE MISS BURDEN does not include a performance license for "Mary's Boy Child" The publisher and author suggest that the licensee contact PRS to ascertain the music publisher and contact such music publisher to license or acquire permission for performance of the song. If a license or permission is unattainable for "Mary's Boy Child" , the licensee may not use the song in LITTLE MISS BURDEN but should create an original composition in a similar style or use a similar song in the public domain. For further information, please see Music Use Note on page iii.

Out of breath **LITTLE MISS** *lies down.*

I'm lying on this bed in a cold corridor.

They've inserted this needle-tubey thing into my hand. It hurts any time I make a fist.

I'm in a dressing gown but not the kind I'd ever wear out. Firstly my bum's exposed and I'm not wearing a bra.

And so I'm covering my chest with my hands so no one sees my pointy nips

MUM They are not the first pair the doctor has seen.

L.M Mum kisses my head and whispers a prayer for me, before the nurse whisks me down the corridor and into the theatre.

I take to the stage for the last time as a ballerina. A farewell performance to the creature I have played for so long, like in Beauty and the Beast the curse has finally been lifted. When I wake I will have returned to human form. Wow there's a lot more people here. I count at least thirteen.

And they were all here for me...

DOCTOR Do you like strawberries?

L.M A very handsome Ana-Anathes-Ana-doctor asks me.

I don't mind them, why?

DOCTOR We're playing with flavoured gas today. I bought you the strawberry flavour.

DOCTOR *places an anaesthesia face mask over* **LITTLE MISS***'s face.*

L.M *(lifts the mask)* Smells more like Calpol.

DOCTOR Fair enough. Now keep it on and count back from hundred for me. I'll start you off.

L.M I can count. Hundred, ninety-nine, ninety-eight, ninety-seven, ninety-six, ninety-five, ninety-four –

DOCTOR – oops didn't push the anaesthetic through. Continue –

L.M – ninety-three, ninety-two, ninety-onnnnneeeee...

Video game warp sound effect[1].

---

1 A license to produce LITTLE MISS BURDEN does not include a performance license for any third-party or copyrighted sound effects. Licensees should create their own.

WORLD 14 - MEMORY LIFT

LITTLE MISS *slides down a tunnel of memories, visions and voices.*

A mix of a boujee nightclub and sensory room.

ANA *holds* **LITTLE MISS***'s hand.*

L.M Who are you?

ANA I'm Anaesthesia but you can call me Ana. Don't let go or you'll float away.

L.M Your palm's really sweaty.

ANA Sorry. Habit. We've all been waiting to meet you. Come on.

ANA *drags* **LITTLE MISS.**

PLASMA Enchanté. Name's Plasma. Think I've seen you around.

L.M Oh yeah. Where you from?

PLASMA All over, where you from?

L.M Hackney.

PLASMA Cool. Cool. I like what they're doing in the area. Used to be so inaccessible and now -

L.M - yeah it's tricky. Cos everything's getting expensive and like family friends are moving away cos they're knocking down their homes.

PLASMA But less stairs, is a good thing right. I'm seeing more coffee shops but also ramps.

L.M I don't drink coffee.

PLASMA Quelle surprise. Neither do I. We have so much in common. Can you feel that...? Feels like a connection between us.

ANA Sorry to interrupt. But I just wanted to introduce you to Brain.

BRAIN Don't be baiting out my government name like that. It's Brian. *(Takes* **LITTLE MISS***'s hand and kisses it)* Pleasure. You're famous *and* infamous fam.

L.M Stop it.

BRAIN I mean it – like seriously – your poetry homework blew my mind -

L.M – I bet you say that to everyone –

BRAIN – the way we came up with *(clears throat) 'he was the reason I took the long way home'*. Sick fam.

L.M Thanks. Appreciate it.

BRAIN But still, so powerful. Like it felt electric just hearing it.

L.M It was a joint effort after all.

BRAIN You know what they say – great minds - will you be looking to publishing it on Bebo maybe or MSN status?

A giant knocking at the door.

Would be good to swap thoughts on Justin Timberlake's success as a solo artist, seems to keep popping up in your dreams –

They try to ignore it but the knocking gets louder.

ANA I'm sorry. I don't know who that'd be...everyone's here, I think.

ANA *lets go of* **LITTLE MISS***'s hand.*

LITTLE MISS *begins to float.*

LGMD Hey, I just wanted to check you knew about the renovations going on. It was quite scary not being informed about it. I'm sorry, am I interrupting something or –

ANA – celebrating our special guest.

LGMD What are you doing here?

L.M I live here.

LGMD What's that *(sniffs)* smells like strawberry air freshener? Wait, so if we're both here, who's out there?

L.M Surgeons.

LGMD They're cutting us open.

L.M No. They're fixing me.

LGMD But we don't need fixing. You're trying to cut me out, aren't you? Is that why you didn't tell me?

ANA Hey-hey, this is a celebratory function, so please adjust your tone.

LGMD And who exactly are you? I've not seen you here before.

ANA Oh sorry, I'm Ana. I organised this little shindig.

LGMD So you're behind this? What the hell! I can't believe I had to find out like this.

PLASMA No biggie mon frère.

ANA You're here now.

BRAIN Yeah bro. Soz you weren't invited. Can I get you a drink?

LGMD Are you fucking kidding me? I live here too. You motherfuckers are trying to evict me.

ANA No one's trying to evict you, we're just trying to clean the house of, you know, any foreign entities...

LGMD And I'm the foreign entity – wow – what does that make her then?

L.M Everyone's welcome, it's fine.

LGMD – that is offensive, you little bitch.

ANA Language. We have a minor in our midst.

LGMD A minor ball ache. She's more foreign than I am – you put her to sleep, that's why you're even here. *(Points to* **LITTLE MISS***)* She didn't get her passport till she was eleven. Did you know that? No you didn't. She was illegal for over a decade.

L.M I was born here.

LGMD *(mimics)* I was born here.

So was I! I've been here since day dot.

PLASMA Oooo la la, calm down. Your temper is hotter than her last fever.

LGMD You can fuck right off.

BRAIN Bro, bro, bro. No need for that, we're all fam here.

LGMD And you can fuck off and all.

L.M Why are you being so aggressive?

LGMD Aggressive? I'll show you aggressive. Babes, this whole affair is pathetic. What exactly are you celebrating? My demise? I ain't going anywhere bitch. You think you can cut me out. I've been here for all your firsts and I'm going to be here for all your lasts.

Video game warp sound effect.[1]

---

1 A license to produce LITTLE MISS BURDEN does not include a performance license for any third-party or copyrighted sound effects. Licensees should create their own.

WORLD 15 – DRIP DROP ISLAND

BIG SIS Queen Mary Hospital, morning

L.M *(groggy)* Rise up this morning...smile with the rising sun

MUM Welcome back *oko mi.*

L.M Mum strokes my face. I can't see hers clearly yet but I could spot Mum's outline anywhere. Groggy and confused. I try to get up to use the toilet but I can't feel my legs.

MUM They asked me what colour you'd like. I think it's too bright but I knew you'd like it.

L.M She pulls back the bed sheet revealing my bright yellow knee-high casts. I smile at her. Then fall back to sleep.

The next morning two eager faces in white T-shirts and trousers greet me in bed. I already knew who they were before they introduced themselves. *(Sniffs)* I recognised that stench of over-enthusiasm anywhere – physiotherapists.

JEN I'm Jen

JANE And I'm Jane

JEN We know you've only just had surgery and it's only been a couple of days but we thought we'd try and get you up on your feet today

JANE The quicker you're able to take steps.

JEN The quicker you can be discharged home.

L.M But I'm in casts, they come up to her knees.

JEN We understand your concern.

JANE We understand.

JEN Yes they are quite thick casts she's got –

JEN/JANE – probably even a little on the heavy side –

JEN – but they have extra padding inside them to allow you to practice walking – you'll need to be able to do that for transfers at home.

JANE From wheelchair to bed

JEN From bed to wheelchair

JANE From wheelchair to toilet

JEN From toilet to wheelchair

JANE From wheelchair to shower

JEN From shower to wheelchair

JANE You get the picture. Right, shall we try getting you up and standing?

JEN Oh yellow, good choice.

JANE I had a blue one when I broke my arm.

JEN So me and Jane are gonna stand either side of you, supporting you under your arms.

JANE When you stand you're going to lean forward towards the walking frame.

JEN OK, ready?

L.M I guess but –

JANE – don't worry it's normal to be a bit scared –

JEN We've got you –

JEN/JANE – we're not going to let you fall –

JEN – you've also got the bed behind you, should you need it.

JANE Ok on three.

JEN One –

JANE – two –

JEN/JANE – three...

Lights down under UV lights. The **SISTERS** *dance to a song in the style of Destiny's Child –* ***"LOSE MY BREATH"***.[1]

JEN Ok ok, you ok?

JANE She's ok.

JEN You ok?

LITTLE MISS *pants.*

We probably should have warned you about the pain.

JANE The general anaesthetic must have worn off

JEN Have you been given any painkillers?

LITTLE MISS *shakes her head.*

Right, ok. We're going to get you some.

JANE Lots... Sorry about that...

JEN We'll try again in a little while.

L.M So how long till I can start running again?

JEN *(checks clipboard)* Oh, says here you had a tendon release

JEN/JANE Ouch

JEN Do you understand what this surgery is for?

L.M To help me walk properly

JEN Yeeess...it should help you walk a little better and be in a little less pain

---

1 A license to produce LITTLE MISS BURDEN does not include a performance license for "Lose My Breath" The publisher and author suggest that the licensee contact PRS to ascertain the music publisher and contact such music publisher to license or acquire permission for performance of the song. If a license or permission is unattainable for "Lose My Breath", the licensee may not use the song in LITTLE MISS BURDEN but should create an original composition in a similar style or use a similar song in the public domain. For further information, please see Music Use Note on page iii.

L.M Didn't the surgery fix me?

JANE What do you mean by fix?

L.M I'm better now. I can run, get off the floor, take part in PE? Now that I can walk properly.

JEN/JANE Oh sweetheart.

JANE I'm sorry if this was never explained to you in a way that you could understand.

JEN Your condition has no cure

JANE No indeedy. Nada.

JEN You're condition is lifelong. You know what that means, right?

JANE Forever

JEN Jane

JANE Jen

JEN Jane

JANE Jen...aren't we just saying each other's name?

LM So I can't run?

JEN If you couldn't run before the surgery

JANE This won't help you to run now

JEN But with treatment like this surgery, we can manage it.

L.M Manage? But I told everyone at school that I'd be –

JEN – great physios like us –

JANE *points to self with her thumbs and a toothy grin.*

– can help you get you back to how you were

JANE With a little more efficiency, conserve a little bit more energy

L.M I don't want to go back to how I was. I want to be better.

JEN We'll go get you some pain meds

JANE Great idea Jen.

JANE *and* **JEN** *exit.*

MUM You are doing so well.

L.M Doesn't feel like it.

MUM You will be able to do so many things for yourself. You won't need me anymore.

L.M I'll still need you...Mum, what if I don't get better?

MUM It will take some time but you will get there.

L.M I have LGMD.

MUM It doesn't have you though.

L.M Sometimes it feels like it does.

MUM Tell me, what does it feel like?

L.M If I'm still and I don't move... I feel like me, just me, but the moment I move it wakes up, like it knows when I'm asleep and awake. It likes to wake up when I want to go to sleep and it wants to go to sleep when I'm trying to stay awake.

MUM You are going to be fine. The surgery was a success. We will celebrate do thanksgiving in Church when you are well. We have a reason to praise the Lord.

WORLD 16 – SHADOW VALLEY

L.M Before I go back to school I'm called in for a check-up with the doctor... My mum's not back yet.

DOCTOR So I can see here you're four months post-op –

L.M – my mum's not back yet –

DOCTOR – you had a tendon release because of your ankle contractures.

L.M I have LGMD.

DOCTOR Oh yeah I've heard of it. And how have you been finding your walking is now?

L.M My heels touch the ground now.

DOCTOR That's what we would expect. And how are you finding getting around?

L.M I'm taller. I've grown half an inch.

DOCTOR Improved posture would do that. What about daily tasks? Do you still require help?

L.M ...Erm. I can brush my teeth myself and get dressed.

DOCTOR How about washing? Cooking? Climbing stairs?

L.M I...my mum helps me.

DOCTOR Have you been receiving physiotherapy?

L.M Yes.

DOCTOR And are you doing them as prescribed?

L.M Yes.

DOCTOR Are you sure?

L.M Yes.

DOCTOR Have you tried doing daily tasks on your own?

L.M Yeah but –

DOCTOR – because you can't expect your mum to help you do everything. Do you want your mum to still be washing and dressing you like a baby?

LITTLE MISS *shakes her head.*

You need to try harder. The surgery was a success, you should be able to do more now, if you have been doing your physiotherapy.

L.M I have.

DOCTOR I'm sure your mum worries a lot about you, so do her a favour and try and pitch in more. It'll benefit you both. Help around the house. Try to find a way you can bathe and cook for yourself. I know how lazy most teenagers are but you're going to be an adult soon. Start behaving like one.

Enter **MUM.**

MUM Sorry doctor. I had to put more money on the meter.

DOCTOR No worries Mum. I was just telling your daughter that I'm happy with her recovery.

DOCTOR *and* **MUM** *disappear and* **LITTLE MISS** *is left alone.*

L.M I don't want to go back to school. I feel sick.

SELIN Oh my God! You're walking so much better.

CJ Loving your boots.

SELIN Looking like a catholic dominatrix.

CJ Are they for your legs?

L.M Sort of. They hide my leg braces.

SELIN So does that mean you're...?

L.M Um...there's something... I need to tell you...

CJ We missed you so much.

SELIN There's so much we have to catch you up on.

L.M *(whispers)* I'm sorry...

CJ What you sorry for?

L.M It didn't work. I'm not fixed.

CJ Did something go wrong?

L.M No...it's me. I'm what's wrong...

CJ Well I'm glad your back.

SELIN Me too.

L.M Everyone's going to find out. The whole school is going to think I'm a liar.

CJ Fuck them. We know you're not.

SELIN You know what you remind me of...a phoenix.

CJ We don't see your disability.

SELIN We see you.

L.M I wish they could see all of me. The staring in school was worse. I hated standing out. I hated how much I disappointed everyone. I hate every step I've climbed. I hate, hate, hate my life!

The door swings open.

LITTLE MISS *goes to close the door but hesitates.*

BIG SIS *and* **LIL' SIS** *are frozen in shock.*

They hear a whistling in the distance.

It's getting louder, she tries to close the door but a gust of wind pins it open.

Hey! I could use some help over here.

LITTLE MISS *shouts for* **BIG SIS** *and* **LIL' SIS** *and they try to close the door but its stuck open like it's glued to the wall.*

BIG SIS Puuuuuuuuuuuuuuuuuuuuuuuuuuusssssssssssshhhhhh hhhhhhhhh!

The whistling is so loud and now accompanied by howls of wind and roars of rain.

LITTLE MISS *realises what the noise is but it's too late.*

L.M TAKE COVER!

FADE She's faking it............Don't want to upset Mum ....becoming a problem............ don't you want to ....make it easier for me........ return it to Mr Satan..................Evil......Cursed...... hunchback.......... liar......... Attention seeker.........You just need to believe......Sinner sinner sinner...I'm sorry.... I'm sorry. I'm sorry... I'm sorry. I'm sorry...pathetic...no wonder you have no friends......disgusting creature like you...No one will ever love you......revolting............Mum doesn't love you............... sisters are tired of you ..... embarrassed by you............ they'd all be happier if you weren't around...... ....It's what Mum wishes........................

.......wouldn't have to explain you.....to anyone...

.........Mum wouldn't be so stressed......

.......so unhappy........so tired..........

So......tired.........so tired......

...........go get lost......................

.......No one wants you....

You're nothing...........

......you're weak.........

..........a waste.......

w

a

s

t

e

o

f

s

p

a

c

e

Words drip on top of **LITTLE MISS***'s head like water from a leaky faucet.*

It is completely dark around her except for the faint light above her head.

FADE *moves into* **LITTLE MISS***'s imagination. Colours fade out.* **FADE** *puts a black and white picture in a frame up on a wall and throws rubbish around.*

You've been having a rough time lately.

L.M Oh great, who are you? Never mind. Everyone is so focused on LGMD, no one will notice the uninvited guest.

FADE You'll have heard of me, I'm a hot topic lately, Depression, but I go by my stage name The Fade.

L.M Take whatever you want. I don't care.

FADE Seems you can't do anything right these days, can you?

L.M I don't want to talk about it.

FADE No worries. I love the sound of my own voice. We're more alike than you and LGMD. Isn't he so annoying?

L.M LGMD has ruined everything. I hate him.

FADE Join the club. He's so selfish.

L.M He is!

FADE And bossy. I don't like the way he talks to you like he was here first.

L.M Exactly! He makes me so angry.

FADE I know. I can feel it. It's powerful.

L.M What?

FADE I feel everything you feel.

L.M Everything?

FADE You have every right to hate LGMD, your sisters, Mum, even God.

L.M I don't hate them.

FADE Why are they normal and not you?

L.M ...Yeah.

FADE What did they do that you didn't?

L.M I don't know what I did.

FADE Must have been bad, since God's punishing you.

L.M I hate going to Church. I hate that Mum makes me pray to a God that doesn't even like me.

FADE You can't trust her or anything she says. She lied to you.

L.M Yeah. She said all I had to do was believe and I'd be fixed. It's worse – I'm worse now.

FADE You know what she's really saying when she prays in Yoruba. She doesn't pray for LGMD to go away. She prays for you to go away.

L.M Really?

FADE You can't trust anyone. They're all liars. God, Mum, your sisters.

L.M You're right.

FADE If everyone agrees you're the problem, then you know what you must do.

L.M Disappear.

FADE You're not a magician. Let's be realistic. You can't do that but we can hide. If people can't see you then...

L.M ...They can't hurt you.

FADE Don't you worry. I'll take it from here. You go hide, I got this.

L.M Thanks.

FADE Remember no talking. We can't trust anyone.

LITTLE MISS *nods.*

Sings.

SO LONG, FAREWELL, AUF WIEDERSEHEN, GOOD NIGHT.

Waving.

Goodbye. Goodbyeeeeeeeeeeeeee.

LITTLE MISS *leaves.*

FADE *opens the door to* **ETTY**.

So glad you could join us. Don't be rude. Introduce yourself.

ETTY *(shy)* Anxiety... Etty for short.

FADE Take off your jacket. Get comfortable.

ETTY I-I like what you've done with the place.

FADE What time is it Etty?

ETTY Erm... I don't have a watch.

FADE It's time to have some fun.

ETTY Can I?

FADE *nods.*

(clears throat) Summer term

FADE Age sixteen

ETTY I-I –

FADE – signing shirts, farewell mass, goodbye assembly, teacher presentations but most importantly. Prom.

ETTY I-I don't want to go to the prom.

FADE Don't worry, neither did she. No one wants her there anyway.

ETTY How about results day?

FADE Doesn't matter, what does she need results for?

ETTY Her summer holiday?

FADE No money. We're broke. Mum's still paying off Nigeria.

ETTY College?

FADE She had to stay on at sixth form.

ETTY She's just sitting there.

FADE That's what we want Etty, we want a goldfish state of mind. We want her to spend the next six weeks watching the world from the bedroom window.

ETTY She's real quiet these days. I like it.

FADE We go to sixth form

ETTY We come straight home

FADE We go to church

ETTY We come straight home

FADE We go to the library

ETTY We come straight home

FADE We sit our A-Levels

ETTY We come straight home

FADE We go to our bedroom

ETTY And we stay there

FADE We stay there

ETTY We sleep there

FADE We cry there

ETTY We eat there

FADE We stay there

ETTY Only there

FADE Forever there

FADE *watches the following exchange with pride.*

MUM Why aren't you dressed? Do you need my help?

L.M ...

MUM I'm talking to you. You are going to be late.

L.M I'm not going.

MUM Why not? It's your first day at university. You can't miss it.

L.M I don't have to.

MUM Says who?

L.M I don't have to go, it's not like college.

MUM You are not going to miss your first day. You almost didn't get in, but by God's mercy He found you a place. *Lo mu'ra.*

L.M How many is it going to take?

MUM How many what?

L.M Prayers, Hail Mary's, Our Fathers? Ten, a hundred, a thousand, ten hundred thousand? So that God forgives me. So that I'm divinely touched. Should I start now? Or do I need to find a desert to get lost in for forty days and forty nights? I don't know any deserts in London, Mum.

MUM You have a medical condition, that's all.

L.M It has a name.

MUM You just have special needs.

L.M What's so special about me? What special powers do I have? What special things can I do? What special language do I speak? I'm not special, Mum. I was never special.

MUM Fine. What do you want me to call you then?

L.M Disabled.

MUM You are not... Look...

MUM *sings a positive song reasurringly.*

L.M Is it? You wouldn't have taken me to all those churches and hospitals and Nigeria, if it was alright. If I was alright.

MUM You are well.

L.M There's a reason why doctors aren't allowed to treat their families, because they don't know when to stop.

MUM You will be well by God's grace.

L.M I don't think I will because let's face it... I. Disgust. God. God doesn't care. If God cared about me then I wouldn't have been born. I wouldn't be like this.

MUM Don't say that. You are exactly how God wanted you to be.

L.M Am I? So I am a monster by design or a mistake? Which one is it?

MUM You are not a monster.

L.M I scare people, Mum. I scare you... I look at myself in the mirror and I can't see it but I know that it sees me. I feel it.

MUM Ah-ah where is this coming from?

L.M Everyone, Mum. Do you know what it's like having to listen to people tell me how much my presence upsets them? I don't even have to say or do anything because everything about me is wrong. The way I look, the way I move, the way I speak, or because of the stuff I can't do. It makes them hate me. And I don't blame them. I'd hate me too. They hate me.

MUM *Ma binu oko mi*, no one hates you.

L.M It's you I blame. You made me this way.

The words hit **MUM** *like a punch to the chest. She is winded and lost for words. She walks away.*

LIL' SIS You really said that to Mum?

LITTLE MISS *nods ashamed.*

BIG SIS I'd have slapped you if you said that to me.

Video game warp sound effect.[1]

---

1 A license to produce LITTLE MISS BURDEN does not include a performance license for any third-party or copyrighted sound effects. Licensees should create their own.

WORLD 17 – FADE INTO YOU

BIG SIS You've not called me in over a month.

L.M (AS FADE) I don't have any credit.

LIL' SIS You've not left your room in ages.

L.M (AS FADE) I don't want to leave.

BIG SIS I've missed hanging out with you.

L.M (AS FADE) Liar. No you haven't.

BIG SIS Mum is worried.

L.M (AS FADE) I'm not doing anything to worry her.

LIL' SIS Come down and have dinner with us.

L.M (AS FADE) I don't want to eat in front of you.

BIG SIS What do you want to do for your birthday? The big one nine.

L.M (AS FADE) No point in celebrating my life.

BIG SIS I haven't seen you for time. Let's go see a film.

L.M (AS FADE) I don't want to leave.

LIL' SIS Come on, it'll be fun.

L.M (AS FADE) I can't leave.

LIL' SIS Fine, then we're going to bring the movies to you.

BIG SIS A la Nollywood style.

Old school dramatic Nollywood music.

BIG SIS *and* **LIL' SIS** *play various characters with Nigerian accents.*

Story Sanctuary Studios presents an international action-packed-romantic-thriller '*Who Ate All The Meat from the Pepper Soup, Leaving Just The Watery Hot Soup?*' –

LIL' SIS – part three!

L.M I'm not playing along.

LIL' SIS Suspense!

BIG SIS So you are not going to deny it *a bi*?

LIL' SIS It wasn't me!

BIG SIS Drama! ...I can smell the pepper on your breath!

L.M Get out! Just leave me alone!

BIG SIS ...We were just getting to the good part.

Enter **MUM.**

MUM *Lowa bi joko si.* I want to have a word with your sister.

BIG SIS/LIL' SIS Yes Mum.

BIG SIS *and* **LIL' SIS** *leave.*

MUM I want to talk with you.

L.M I'm sorry for what I said to you, but I don't want to talk.

MUM It's ok. I know you were upset. How long are you going to stay in here?

L.M ...

MUM This is not what I want for you. Not going out, ignoring your studies, not smiling, not speaking to your family. Your future is not in this room... Talk to me.

L.M I'm done trying. I'm done.

MUM You are too young to be done.

L.M Whatever... this is my life now.

MUM You know, growing up in Nigeria, we believe there's nothing prayer cannot answer. The tongue has power, anything you want or need, you must speak it into existence. Prayer is about taking charge of one's destiny.

L.M I used to imagine prayers went up to God like paper lanterns. Slowly, sometimes they could get blown off course, but they'd make it there eventually. But some prayers, like mine, would burn to ashes and float back to earth. Like a missed call.

MUM God hears all prayers.

L.M Well I've stopped praying because every time you, or a pastor, say God will heal me, it hurts because it sounds like you blame me. Like I'm doing something wrong. Like I'm the one preventing some miracle from happening.

MUM I don't blame you. I have never blamed you. Prayer is what I need but maybe prayer is not what you need. I think it would be good for you to speak to someone.

L.M No, I'm good.

MUM Talking about how your condition makes you feel to someone impartial could help. I know there are some things you won't want to tell me but you need to tell somebody.

L.M I'll think about it.

MUM No one knows the future, no doctor or pastor can tell us what is to come but we can find ways for you to cope.

L.M Cope?

MUM With being a young, intelligent, black, disabled woman in this world.

L.M I'm disabled?

MUM You are and you are also my daughter and you are made in God's image. You are not what I expected, you are better than I could have ever hoped for. You are extraordinary.

L.M You have to say that, you're my mum.

MUM I will share this prayer of mine with you. For you and your sisters, I always pray that God continues to strengthen your resilience and that He blesses you with abundant happiness throughout your life. You will find your happy place in this world and find people who love you even more than I do... say amen.

L.M Amen.

MUM Not you.

LGMD ...Amen.

WORLD 18 – WORDS! HAVE! POWER!

L.M Come here.

LGMD Why? You going to berate me, say you hate me. Wish I hadn't been born.

L.M No.

LGMD You going to apologise?

L.M Apologise? When you're the one – you know what, I'm done arguing.

LGMD What do you want?

L.M We've been offered a very unique opportunity to go on an adventure.

LGMD Oh yeah, so why are you consulting me? You're the boss I'm just a temp, remember.

L.M You know, you're not a temp. I wish you were a temp, you're permanent staff. So we're going away.

LGMD Where?

L.M Do you trust me?

LGMD Are you trying to get rid of me again?

L.M No. But I can't go without you and you can't stay here without me.

LGMD Does Mum know about this? I'm not hiding this from her.

L.M She knows. They all know.

MUM You will only be a two hour flight away. If anything happens I will come and bring you back home myself.

L.M It'll just be me and you.

LGMD I can't believe this. I don't even get a say now.

L.M You're literally the reason I'm eligible to go in the first place. If you don't want to go just say so and we won't.

LGMD I'm just being cautious.

L.M Well, I'm making an executive decision. We're going. You don't have to be afraid.

LGMD I'm a rare disease for a reason. I fear no one.

L.M For the sake of the trip, it's important we call a truce. We have a mutual enemy on board who I don't think likes either of us. And the enemy of my enemy can be a colleague.

LGMD I don't think that's how the saying goes.

L.M *(sighs exasperatedly)* For that week, no more fighting or sneaky tactics.

LGMD You're no fun.

L.M I'm serious. I'm not going to fight you.

LGMD Then I win then.

L.M There aren't any winners or losers just a ship and I'm looking for an ally to run this ship. Whilst I steer, you be lookout and when you steer I'll be lookout. After all we both want the same thing.

L.M/LGMD To live.

LGMD I don't want to be treated like a passenger. I want to co-captain.

L.M Fine. We share this body then.

LGMD I don't share. I own.

L.M If you want to own this slap, I'd suggest you cooperate.

LGMD There you go with the intimidation and we've not even left yet.

L.M Look... I think we're a lot more similar than you think. We both have siblings, we're both like dancing, I like hip-hop, you ballet, we both hate cold weather and are strategic, practical thinkers, and we both love her. We can't live without her.

LGMD Impossible. Who wouldn't love her in their lives?

L.M I think we just agreed on something. So how are we going to do this?

LGMD Firstly you can start by calling me Limmy G.

L.M I'm not calling you that.

LGMD Fine. Do the thing.

L.M What thing?

LGMD The thing they do.

L.M Oh.

LITTLE MISS *snaps her fingers.*

LIL' SIS You rang?

BIG SIS What? You ready to finish the story now?

L.M Yeah, but I kind of want to do it a little differently.

BIG SIS Lucky you're related to some strong improvisers.

LIL' SIS *(in a super posh accent)* Didn't you know we were classically trained darling? I can do an authentic African accent.

BIG SIS Oh yeah, you can do an accent from all 54 countries or just the five hundred and twenty languages spoken in Nigeria?

LIL' SIS ...Places.

BIG SIS Heathrow

LIL' SIS Age twenty

LGMD Tignes, France

LIL' SIS It's minus three degrees –

L.M – and we're at a resort at a four star hotel. I'm ruined. I will never stay in anything less.

LGMD We're on an all-expenses paid –

BIG SIS – winter sports retreat –

L.M – for disabled adults –

LGMD – recommended by our therapist.

L.M Yeah. Therapy is hard but it's how we keep our head above water.

LGMD We're surrounded by five inches of snow.

L.M It takes two volunteers to push us in our manual wheelchair through the snow.

LGMD We use a wheelchair now, deal with it.

L.M Beth and Katerina are physiotherapists – Katerina runs the charity with her competitive wheelchair tennis player husband.

LIL' SIS He's very handsome.

LGMD And a daredevil.

L.M He's so fearless. How does he do that?

BIG SIS *and* **LIL' SIS** *behave like characters from video game.*

LGMD They stop the ski lift to give us a chance to sit on the bench.

L.M They lock us in place with a metal brace as we cling on for dear life as we're lifted above the ground.

CONTROL Your mission is to get to the bottom of the mountain collecting as many rings as you can before the Avalanche of Assumptions submerges you and everyone in the resort under its weight of judgement. God speed.

L.M We look up, taking in the crisp morning air and piercing sun.

LGMD We put on our goggles.

L.M Rub extra sun cream on our nose.

LGMD We're over two thousand feet up this snow covered mountain.

L.M The world beneath our sit-ski.

BIG SIS/LIL' SIS Allez gros!

L.M Down the mountain we glide. Leaning left and right in our sit-ski to control our speed.

LGMD Our instructor blasting bazookas to ward off the Fade's minions.

BIG SIS *mimes loading a bazooka and firing it, blasting* **LIL' SIS** *to smithereens.*

L.M We're skiing through a postcard-esque landscape.

LGMD The kind that's so pleasing to look at you forget to blink.

L.M The resort not yet in sight, we shout to our instructor *jeûneur*.

LGMD We lean even deeper left then deeper right.

L.M We pick up speed.

LGMD I look behind us and see the roar of the Avalanche racing toward us.

L.M Right. Left. Right. Left. We spot another of The Fade's minions, Etty..

LGMD Instructor! Bazooka that bitch.

L.M Boom! And Etty is taken out. Dissolving into the snow.

LGMD Right. Left. Right. Left.

L.M The Avalanche of Assumptions is gaining on us, screeching ever closer and louder like an eagle clawing at our ear drums.

LGMD Droite. La gauche. Droite. La gauche.

L.M I can make out the resort in the distance. I can see the chequered finish line.

LGMD Right. Left. Right. Left.

L.M But out of nowhere, we spot a physio-yeti's, its paws grab at our sit-ski.

LGMD We successfully swerve around its grabs and collect confidence coins.

L.M We're skiing. We're really skiing down a mountain.

LGMD We're skiing together in Tignes.

L.M And around its one last lean –

L.M/LGMD Riiiiiiiigggghhhhhhhttttt!

A video game misson accomplished sound effect plays. [1]

They pose for a photo. Flash!

L.M Our sit-ski tips over onto its side.

LGMD But it's ok, because we did it!

L.M Why are you shouting?

LGMD Because it's still so loud.

L.M That's our heart.

LGMD What is this feeling?!

L.M Adrenaline...

LGMD We've never felt like this before.

L.M It feels so alive. Everything is awake. Especially our bladder.

LGMD We feel invincible...

---

1 A license to produce LITTLE MISS BURDEN does not include a performance license for any third-party or copyrighted sound effects. Licensees should create their own.

*A song in the style of Vanessa Da Mata & Ben Harper – **"BOA SORTE (GOOD LUCK)"**[2] fades in, the way a good memory does.*

L.M We spend the week at the resort doing everything.

LGMD Whilst not climbing a single step.

BIG SIS They stay on the fifth floor in a completely wheelchair accessible room. *(Collects gold ring)*

L.M It has a comfier bed than the one we sleep on at home. *(Collects gold ring)*

LIL' SIS They ride a snowmobile up a mountain to a rustic restaurant. *(Collects gold ring)*

L.M Whilst riding, we hear snow. Have you ever heard snow before? It's incredible. We're both in awe. I didn't – we didn't know this was possible, that we could be here. *(Collects gold ring)*

BIG SIS They try espresso for the first and last time.

L.M It's an acquired taste. *(Collects gold ring)*

LGMD We're not keen drinkers but we try some expensive wine. *(Collects gold ring)*

LIL' SIS They visit their first night club. *(Collects gold ring)*

LGMD During the day.

L.M Up another mountain. There are lots of mountains in Tignes.

BIG SIS In minus twenty-two degree weather

---

2 A license to produce LITTLE MISS BURDEN does not include a performance license for "Boa Sorte (Good Luck)" The publisher and author suggest that the licensee contact PRS to ascertain the music publisher and contact such music publisher to license or acquire permission for performance of the song. If a license or permission is unattainable for "Boa Sorte (Good Luck)", the licensee may not use the song in LITTLE MISS BURDEN but should create an original composition in a similar style or use a similar song in the public domain. For further information, please see Music Use Note on page iii.

LIL' SIS Where you had to dance to stay warm

L.M And alive

The music turns up. A dancing **LITTLE MISS** *locks eyes with a handsome stranger at the bar.*

JEAN Can I get you a drink?

L.M Nah.

JEAN Why not?

L.M Because I'm getting you one.

JEAN What's your name?

L.M Little Miss.

JEAN Unique... I like.

L.M I know.

JEAN Can I get your number?

L.M Only if you race me down the mountain... and win.

LGMD We are lifted up flights of stairs

L.M We ride in a cable car and smash through clouds.

LGMD We did all that together

L.M When we came back home we weren't the same.

LGMD Our sight had changed

L.M COLOUR has been restored.

Colours flood the stage.

Turns out there is so much we are capable of, when obstacles are removed.

An upbeat song is played.

L.M *(holds up a pen like a sceptre)* Words! Have! Power!

LGMD For the next two years our therapist helped her understand that she could share a life with me and it not be tragic.

L.M I don't have to like it.

LGMD Hey! I thought we were getting close.

L.M We're already too close. We learn to communicate more, accept help when we need it and ask for help when we require it.

LGMD We are deserving of help.

L.M Counselling revealed that there are more sides to me than a decagon.

BIG SIS The term for a ten-sided shape, think a large pizza for those who failed GCSE maths.

L.M My disability just happens to be a prominent slice, without which I wouldn't be whole.

LGMD So we don't drop out of university

L.M And I find my voice on the page

LIL' SIS Hold on, best bits coming up.

ALL Sailor Venus. Sailor Mercury. Sailor Mars. Sailor Jupiter.

L.M Sailor Moon has Sailor Scouts. And I have Sailor Sisters to help me slay the real monsters out there.

BIG SIS Because trust, there's a lot of them out there.

LIL' SIS And some of them run countries.

L.M I must always remember that I am not the symptoms of LGMD.

LGMD That's my job.

L.M I'm not weak, a waste, or a disease.

LGMD I prefer the term mutant.

L.M I realise the power words have. They are the battery packs to my thoughts.

L.M The right words could light up a whole new world.

I hail from a tribe of women taking charge of their destinies whatever their circumstance and I am learning to take great pride in that. Because I get to experience all of my selves through the magical plane of stories.

L.M This is my story.

L.M And with my Sailor Scouts behind me, there's hope.

The **SISTERS** *break into a dance routine in the style of India Arie –* ***"THERE'S HOPE"***[1] *but they've switched up the last line of the chorus for* **LITTLE MISS.**

BIG SIS Whenever you hear this song, it is a reminder that we are here for you. Always.

LIL' SIS And you are here for us.

L.M Always

The **SISTERS** *dance out the rest of the song together.*

Soft blackout but the dancing still continues.

---

1 A license to produce LITTLE MISS BURDEN does not include a performance license for "There's Hope" The publisher and author suggest that the licensee contact PRS to ascertain the music publisher and contact such music publisher to license or acquire permission for performance of the song. If a license or permission is unattainable for "There's Hope", the licensee may not use the song in LITTLE MISS BURDEN but should create an original composition in a similar style or use a similar song in the public domain. For further information, please see Music Use Note on page iii.

RUBBLE OF RUBIES

Lights up. We're not performing now. We are in the real world and there are things that need to be said.

L.M There are rights that have not been written into law...yet... for people like me

BIG SIS But we know them to be true and just

L.M They may well never be written into law but they do exist. These rights are yours and you must defend them.

BIG SIS But you don't have to do it alone

L.M These rights must be protected.

LIL' SIS These rights must be uttered

BIG SIS These rights must be heard

L.M You have the right to remain loud

BIG SIS And proud

L.M You have the right to take up space

LIL' SIS On a bus

BIG SIS On a train

LIL' SIS On a plane

L.M You have the right to a world built for you

BIG SIS And not against you

L.M You have the right to have sex

BIG SIS Safe sex

LIL' SIS Good sex

L.M Great sex

LIL' SIS Frequent sex

BIG SIS Let's just agree lots and lots of sex

L.M You have the right to love and be loved

LIL' SIS To intimacy

BIG SIS And privacy

L.M You have the right to not be grateful

LIL' SIS Or thankful

BIG SIS Or any other thing-ful

L.M You have a right to dignity

LIL' SIS And respect

L.M You have the right to earn

BIG SIS And learn

L.M You have the right to choose

BIG SIS Your bedtime

L.M You have the right to choose

LIL' SIS A lifetime

L.M You have the right to just choose

BIG SIS And not apologise

L.M You have the right to friendship

BIG SIS Leadership

LIL' SIS All kinds of relationships

L.M You have the right to create dreams

LIL' SIS To plant seeds

BIG SIS And watch them grow

L.M You have the right to be fucking sad

LIL' SIS Screaming mad

L.M You have the right to say no

BIG SIS Hell no

LIL' SIS Fuck no

L.M You have the right to not be patient

BIG SIS Or polite

LIL' SIS Or passive

L.M You have the right to find yourself

BIG SIS Feel yourself

LIL' SIS See yourself

L.M Demand more for yourself
You have the right, to just fucking be
You have the right, to just fucking be
You have the right, to just...fucking...be

Blackout.

YORUBA GLOSSARY

HAIRSTYLES

Ko l'ese – no legs
Ipako elede – pigs head
Suku – closely weaved gourd
Pa nu mo – closed mouth (also colloquialism for 'shut up')
Suku ologede – closely weaved like a banana
Biba – single plaits

Okele – staple food - a thick starchy paste (e.g. pounded yam, ébà, àmàlà) which is then eaten with soups or sauces.

Mimo - Holy

Amin Jesu – Amen in Jesus' name

Oloshi – Idiot

Oko mi – My darling

Se o gbo Yoruba? – Do you understand Yoruba?

Agbada – a flowing wide-sleeved robe worn by men in much of West Africa, a Yoruba variant to the dashiki. In northern Nigeria it's called babariga.

Oluwa lon fun ogbon, ki se eniyan – God gives us wisdom not man.

Kabiyesi Olodumare – Almighty God – Kabiyesi is the greeting for a king. It's like saying, Your Majesty.

Ewe nje ogun ti o je ewe ni o pe – Herbs that do not work means the recipe is not complete.

Agbo ti o n mu yi a tu e lara – The herbs you are drinking will bring you relief.

Omo ki i ku l'owo onikola – A child does not die while being cared for.

Àjèjé owo kan ko gbe igbá de ori – You cannot lift up a load and place it onto your head with one hand.

War in bi Olorun se da e – You will walk, as God has made you.

Ara a tu e – You will be healed

Oluwa şeun – Thank God.

Ma binu oko mi – Don't be upset, my darling.

Lo mu'ra – Go get ready

Lowa bi joko si – Go and sit down somewhere

Jedi jedi – Herbal medicine

Lightning Source UK Ltd.
Milton Keynes UK
UKHW020220121219
355186UK00006B/316/P

9 780573 130175